Arianrhod's Dance

Also available from Grey House in the Woods

the Voice within the Wind
of Becoming and the Druid Way
Greywind

the Path through the Forest - a Druid Guidebook
Julie White & Graeme K Talboys

Forthcoming titles

Wealden Hill
a novel
Graeme K Talboys

Answers To Some Questions You Are Likely To Be Asked If You
Tell Someone You Are Druid
Graeme K Talboys & Julie White

The cover of this book depicts a set of eight standing stones encircling the Earth. All the symbols used are well known and ancient. The phases of the Moon are self-evident. The use of three concentric circles to depict the solar cycle is well attested, the inner circle being the winter solstice, the middle circle the equinoxes, and the outer circle the summer solstice. The Beltane symbol is Pictish and represents the cauldron. The set is oriented to the East, just as our ancestors saw the world – facing the Sun as it rose each day.

Arianrhod's Dance
a
Druid Ritual Handbook

Julie White
&
Graeme K Talboys

Grey House in the Woods

First published in 2004 by
Grey House in the Woods
PO Box 8211
Girvan
Ayrshire
KA26 0WA
Scotland

ISBN 0-9540531-2-5

Cover design by Greywind
Design consultant - Redwind

Set in 9-point Comic Sans MS

CONTENTS

Arianrhod's Dance is dedicated
to
the memory
of
HARLEY
beloved companion
exploring the Otherworld
and sorely missed in this

you may wonder
for a hundred lifetimes
each of a hundred years
whilst the stars wheel
and the land bears fruit
and the bonny streams sing

you may study
for a thousand millennia
at the feet of sages
whilst the stars dim
and the land grows tired
and the seas grow still

you may watch
for the lifetime of the gods
and the goddesses who nurtured them
whilst the stars are reborn
and new lands arise
and rain falls once more

but

you will never tell
the dancer from the dance

ACKNOWLEDGEMENTS

The writers of any book know that their thoughts and words are shaped by the companions that surround them and the land in which they dwell, as well as the other forces that play more lightly about their lives.

Julie would like to give special thanks to and for:
Arianrhod, Goddess of the Silver Wheel;
the South Downs and the Seashore;
Selene - my beautiful daughter;
Vic - my partner;
Harley - my devoted dog;
Graeme - my dear friend who has given me the confidence to call myself a writer;
and Maddy, Beth, and Kate for always listening.

Graeme would like to give special thanks to and for:
Myrddin – to whom I turn for inspiration and understanding;
the flint blue vision of Avallach;
Barbara – my strength and my love;
Catkin and Matilda – whom we all obey without question;
Julie – a true friend and a dancer who has opened to me parts of the Forest I would otherwise never have known;
and all those dear friends who have had faith in my work and shone light into the gloom – new companions of the Silver Star.

We would both like to thank:
Faulks Books and Grey House in the Woods for their support and infinite patience.

PREFACE

This book, a companion to *the Path through the Forest*, is about the ways in which we celebrate the events of our lives. It explains something of what ceremony, ritual, and prayer consist in and why they are important. It also offers an introduction to the meaning of specific ceremonies, as well as offering rituals that can be used by Hedge Druids and Groves alike.

The content is not comprehensive by any means, not least because the rituals herein are only suggestions; but also because the insights one can gain from meditating on and enacting ceremonies are infinite. All we intend here is to guide you to some basic forms, which you can use, adapt, and evolve to suit your own path through the Forest.

That said, everything that follows is well considered and based, where possible, on what very little we know of historical material and practice. They are, in all cases, tried and tested. We hope that you find them both useful and enjoyable, and that they provide a solid working base for the development of your own approach to ceremony, ritual, and prayer.

This may seem daunting at the outset, but if you take things carefully and slowly, the ritual aspect of your life will soon come naturally. You will then be able to enter deeply into the spirit of the work you do, whereupon you will discover that in those depths is to be found great joy.

Please note that parts of 'Casting a Circle and Circle Working' are also to be found in *the Path through the Forest*. We make no apology for this. Although the books were written as companion pieces, we wanted each to stand alone and these sections rightly belong in both volumes.

Julie White
Graeme K Talboys

CEREMONY, RITUAL, AND PRAYER

For Druids, everything they are and do is informed by the rhythms of the Land, the Sea, and the Sky. These are the slow beating of our spiritual heart, the multi-dimensional frame on which we hang the rich tapestry of our being.

Our recognition of this is marked by an annual round of ceremonies. Some are fixed events, working with the dance of Sun, Moon, and Stars. Others are more intimate rituals, determined not only by the major events of our lives but also accompanying the daily and mundane activities that we undertake.

There is, of course, a great deal more to being Druid than performing rituals. Indeed, many Druids, whilst recognizing the importance of these events, do not make a great song and dance of them. Hedge Druids in particular often mark the important times with quiet periods of meditation and simple ritual rather than elaborate ceremony. Yet, in whatever way these events are approached, the underlying spirit and the intent are the same, for celebration is both important and integral to the Druid Way.

The act of celebration through ritual is, of course, one of the major means by which we integrate the material and spiritual aspects of our lives. In the most obvious and overt way, we use material objects and physical expression to create a space in which we can focus on the spiritual.

For Druids (and for many other pagans), this space is delineated not by a formal structure, but by the drawing of a circle at the place we have chosen for the ritual. Strictly speaking, we work within a sphere. This is discussed in the next chapter, but as the casting of a circle creates a sphere and we move in circles within it, it is easier to continue talking of a circle.

The symbolism of the circle is discussed briefly in *the Path through the Forest*, yet the circle is important for more than its symbolic value. The physical shape in the material world, even if it is drawn in the air or the mind, is a powerful presence. What is more, in keeping with all that Druids hold sacred, it is temporary. No matter what positive energies may radiate from the ritual performed within, the circle is always closed at the finish and the place of ritual is left as if no one had been there.

The circle is a shape in which thought, light, and other energies radiate evenly from the centre and it is one in which all who form the shape are of equal standing. What is more, a circle is easy to

5

draw. As a physical presence, a single person simply needs to turn on the spot, marking the ground with a stick or staff; a group can hold hands and spread out evenly. Many experienced practitioners who work alone often envisage a circle in their mind, which is far easier to imagine and hold there than any other shape.

The creation of this space is a first and simple step that uses the material to bring thought and action to bear on the spiritual. However, the integration of these aspects of our being goes much further than this. We do not simply use the one to gain enhanced engagement with the other. Rather we work within the space we have created to move onward, using the aspect of our being in which we are deeply seated (the material) in order to secure our integration with that aspect of our being to which we strongly aspire (the spiritual). As in all things, we strive for balance.

Of course, we must not assume that we are any more familiar or at ease with our material selves than we are with our spiritual. Quite aside from the fact that we rarely consider the two aspects to be manifestations of a unified being, we often treat our material selves with a great deal of contempt. Our ancestors took care of their bodies as much as they took care of their souls. This was not out of vanity, but out of a recognition that body and soul are one and that the welfare of both is important.

The shape of ritual is also important. Each one has evolved complex, multi-layered forms that entrain the whole being, opening us up within protected space to the wider existence of which we are a part. The objects used, the words spoken, and the physical actions - all act as triggers. Their cumulative effect is profound as they become imbued with universal and personal symbolic significance, working as keys to unlock those aspects of our being that need constant release.

The more we enact a given ritual, the more we are able to concentrate on content and meaning rather than form. We journey through the years from the material and formal expression into the underlying principles on which these are based. This is not to say that form is unimportant. Far from it. The formal shape of ritual is the hearth from which we journey and which remains as a haven to which we may return. However, we must journey away from the hearth if we are to discover its importance. We must journey away if we are, ultimately, to return. That is why we have kept the rituals in this book as simple as possible. If you concentrate too much on form, the ritual is quite literally meaningless. The journey never begins.

The form also has importance because it is in the repetition and in the use of specific objects that we build up the associations and charge the symbols that unlock the mystery within. There is a balance to be kept here as elsewhere. Too much emphasis on the material aspect and it becomes a habit, a chore, something to be cast aside. But if the material is wholly cast aside in favour of a simple meditation, then it ceases to be the specific and special ritual or ceremony that is essential - be it to celebrating the turning of the year or the cycle of life.

A further facet of this is that whilst meditation alone does not constitute a full and specific ritual, performing ritual on a regular basis *is* a form of meditation. Moreover, as with all meditation, the more it is practised, the easier it becomes, the more it is of benefit.

With Druid meditation, we do not try to attain a state of disconnectedness. Rather, we focus on particular symbols and myth cycles, as well as deities and entities, in order to reach a deeper understanding of and more profound connection with the worlds we inhabit. The rituals that mark the turning of the year, the rites of passage, along with any other rituals we choose to perform (welcoming the day, honouring the quarters of the moon, and so on) are themselves hugely complex and living symbols that contain pointers to myth and deity. Enacting these on a regular basis is much the same in the long term (although on a much larger scale) as sitting down each day for a short, personal meditation.

In terms of effect, however, there is a great difference. Much as each ritual itself unites the material and spiritual aspects of our lives, the cumulative effect of a lifetime of ritual is to generate a calming and ordering of the environment in which the rituals take place.

This is not simply the physical environment. If you carry out your rituals in a particular place, it has a beneficial effect on that location. However, the effect is in time and it is in spirit as well. Continuity over a long period creates a sacred place and space within and from which the Hedge Druid or Grove can work. And not only does this enhance their own being, but it also works through them to enhance the worlds they inhabit.

The place of ritual itself becomes a centre of harmony and a source of power. It is protected. It is calm. This has a beneficial effect on the surrounding plants and animals and radiates beyond that into the contiguous spiritual and material planes in both space and time. It also works inward into the environments of our person, balancing our inner ecologies.

Through this action of long-term meditative work, ritual also aligns those who undertake it with, and opens them up to, the basic energies of the universe. This is not, however, for the purpose of empowerment. Druids do not work for aggrandizement. They work to become conduits by which the healing energies of the universe can be applied to the hurts of the world. Nor is this a matter of blind channelling. It must be done with intelligence and right intent.

The meditative effect of ritual is to make one supremely aware of the connection between the material and the spiritual aspects of our being. It guides us to the realization that the material and spiritual are not separate, merely the same thing seen from a different perspective. That the spirit is withered in many of us is another matter altogether and part of the larger work of being Druid. However, ritual is an important method by which our spirit is nurtured. It also provides us with a disciplined approach through which our openness to the universe is guided by the wisdom inherent in the structure of ritual.

Such grand sounding intent would seem to imply that all ceremony is a matter of gravity and pomp - robes and paraphernalia, obscure rites and archaic language. This is not the case. Ceremony can be enacted simply and alone or in small groups, and it is often more appropriate to do so. Formal events have their place, but just as we cannot always live on a mystical high, so we cannot always approach our veneration of the worlds in a formal way. We must learn to touch and appreciate all the worlds in an intimate fashion. Formal courtship must always be accompanied with informal companionship if a genuine relationship between our own being and the worlds we inhabit is to develop.

This more intimate approach is often accomplished through prayer. Prayer is problematic for many pagans. They see it as belonging largely to Judaism, Christianity, and Islam - none of which have any degree of sympathy for paganism. However, prayer is much older than these desert faiths and we all indulge in it, quite often without realizing. Pleading with a recalcitrant car to start on a cold morning, touching wood or throwing coins into water for luck, taking our mascot (often a quasi-totem animal) into an exam – these are all forms of prayer.

Prayer works in much the same way as more formal ritual, except that it rarely takes place within specially created sacred space. Rather, it is the daily conversation we have with the sacred that is all about us. That it is a conversation is important to remember. There are two sides to it and whilst we are all very good at our side, when it comes to listening to what the world has to tell us, many of us have closed ears.

One of the things we must all learn as Druids is how to open our ears to the other side of the conversation; and to learn that our 'ears' are not always those things on the side of our heads. Ever heard a little voice inside, somewhere, which urges you to do or not do something? Ever found a journey starting out disastrously with missed buses and forgotten purses and a headache? And, when you get to the other end, you have a dismal time? You should have listened.

It is important to listen, because the world about us is our greatest teacher. Druids are not made by reading books (although they certainly help in the absence of Druid colleges and mentors). Druids are made by learning to see (rather than just look) and learning to listen (rather than just hear). They are made by engaging with the world, with the sacred.

Prayer is a method of training in that, as well as a way of keeping up the conversation. It is, in fact, the way in which we attune ourselves to the everyday. And the everyday is so very important, for it is in the everyday that true magic is to be found – in the growing of food, in cooking, in companionship, in the simple sights, sounds, and experiences of our lives. Therein lies the majesty and wonder of the universe for whilst such as the stars are a great glory, we cannot touch them; merely watch them from a distance.

It is clear, then, that one of the purposes and results of ritual is unity. Ritual enables us to unify our lives, as we must bring all aspects of our being to bear on a single focus. We must concentrate all that we are into a single event. If done properly, this unification stays with us once the circle is closed. It becomes habitual in the sense that we live within it.

This is important. Ritual, like mystical experience, is of necessity short lived. Our physical bodies could not stand the strain of constant ecstasy, of constant focus. This was recognized by those who told the Grail stories. Those who achieved the Grail, died as a result. The physical bodies of even the strongest and battle-hardened knights could not withstand the constant presence of mystical understanding.

This is not to say that we are not changed by enlightenment. We are. However, life goes on - a life lived in a new way with different priorities. This is because we perceive the world in a new and more comprehensive way, with the lessons learned from our brief glimpses of the infinite carried with us into our everyday lives. Indeed, that is the point of ritual, the point of seeking the mysteries. They are not ends in themselves, but a means to an end.

Our lives are unified by the actions we take and the journeys we make. We integrate the spiritual with the material, the everyday with the infinite, the mundane with the mystical. It enables us to see ourselves as we really are, which is a whole being rather than disparate parts. We may continue to wear different hats but, beneath the hats, we become less fragmented, less stressed, less uncertain of our direction. Eventually we feel no need for hats at all.

Unity does not confine itself to each person becoming more integrated within themselves. Ritual also acts to help each person unify their self with the rest of creation. One of the greatest problems facing humanity is a false belief that we are somehow separate from the rest of the world. The reasons for this attitude are historically and philosophically complex and do not come within the scope of this book. However, ritual is an excellent means by which we can alter our mindset and create a new metaphysic that accepts the fact that people are just a small part of an enormous whole.

We cannot unify ourselves through ritual without also unifying ourselves with all with which we come into contact. As ritual creates sacred space, which is a focus for all aspects of existence, we place ourselves into a situation where we have to integrate or accept that ritual is pointless.

It is one of the mysteries of such experience that whilst we recognize we are each infinitesimal on a universal scale, we also understand that we do exist and we do have a place. We are part of the song and without it, the song would be lessened, just as the absence of a sparrow, or a blade of grass, or a tree, or a drop of rain would lessen it.

Ritual also plays its part in this understanding. It integrates us with the universe, but it also enables us to celebrate our uniqueness. As Druids, we celebrate in a particular way. As individual Druids, we each adapt the form of celebration to suit our own circumstance and understanding.

Our rituals are part of us and develop with us. They allow us to express ourselves in ways true to our own nature whilst also celebrating the ineffable. We each react to the mysteries and to our own development in ways that we should celebrate. It is a dimension that is often overlooked in ritual. The intent may be serious and profound, we may be dealing with mysteries and intense emotional experiences, but we should take joy in that. We should take joy in the very fact that we can celebrate and that we each have our own way of doing it.

All things celebrate their existence in their own way; take joy in their very being. Birds tumble on gusty winds and skim the waves simply because they can. Dolphins and whales leap for the sheer joy of it. Cows play because the sun is shining. Wild flowers paint the meadows because it is a joyous use of daylight. All things may have mechanistic reasons for being, but that does not mean they are not also celebratory. The mundane is also the wonderful. Each simple action of our being, especially those born of unconscious joy in something, is one of celebration.

Ritual, therefore, is a way of celebrating our own existence; it is a way of recognizing our own dance. And no matter how small that dance may be, ritual allows us to recognize also that we each do have a part to play. It allows us to consider how we are playing that part and how we might better be serving the world.

Once again, this occurs not just within the ritual. The symbols we use are not confined or confinable to the sacred space. By marking specific times of the year and specific events in our lives, we continue to open the doors that release our potential, that release our spirit, that release our understanding.

The annual rituals make use of myth and of deity, but they do not make use of it all. Nor do they confine it. They act as a focus. They revitalize us, make us think about specific things, but they also add to what we learned last time round.

11

Each ritual is like a beacon lit upon a hilltop. We can dance within its warmth, gather within its light, and enjoy it while it is there. However, when the flames have died down, we go about our lives with a memory of them illuminating the rest of what we do. They are spiritual lighthouses guiding us and casting light upon the whole cycle of myth that aids our understanding of the many worlds in which we live and of the life that we live within them.

We can extend that celebration beyond ritual by allowing the lessons we learn to be applied to the rest of our lives. Everyday actions and activities should carry with them the sacred, even cleaning and shopping. In addition, there are many practical ways in which we can express our joy - for example, by helping animals or becoming involved in conservation work. From very small acts of thanks (for a meal or a task completed) through to the major celebrations (such as burial and memorial ceremonies), both the impulse and the result are the same.

It is important to recognize that the celebrations given in this book are, in themselves, different aspects of a unified celebration of our very existence. Although each one focuses on a different aspect of our life and its connection with the rest of existence, they are part of a larger pattern which sees them not as something special (although they undoubtedly are), but as something essential to right living.

CASTING A CIRCLE AND CIRCLE WORKING

The importance of the circle

To cast a circle is to create sacred space - a place between the worlds and beyond the boundaries of time and space. When we cast a circle, we build an energy circuit with which to work. It contains certain forces and keeps others out.

The act of casting a circle resounds far beyond the two-dimensional figure that is traced upon the ground. In fact, we actually create a multi-dimensional sphere, one that encloses us entirely in all the worlds and which, as a result, provides access to those worlds. Whilst we might consider the necessary complexity of this in meditation, it is far easier in practice to refer to this space as a circle.

Within such a circle, different rules apply from those of the everyday world. We are in meta-time, working at nature's pace. We are in a place that borders all the worlds where we can perform our rituals and enact our meditations – channelling energies from all sources and working with them on physical, mental, and psychic levels. It is where we meet the Goddess and God.

Our ancestors who built the great stone circles probably did not cast as we do today. The priesthood at the time would presumably have enacted rituals at these sites. The energies produced would have built up over hundreds of years, stored within the structure, so getting rid of the need to cast each circle anew. But this is speculation.

The content and practice of ancestral Druid ritual is equally obscure. There is, of course, clear evidence that Druids worked in a circle, or an oval shape. They used circular groves of oak and yew, and maybe even built some stone circles of their own. Whatever the case, the circle was important to them at a symbolic, ritual, and magical level.

They saw the universe as a circle and the circle as the universe. The sky was round as they studied the stars, the Earth was round as they studied the horizon. The Sun and the Moon were not only circles of light, but also travelled on a circular route through the cosmos, which in turn brought about day and night, light and dark, heat and cold. Indeed, the circle symbolized life, death, and re-birth itself.

Today we work in a slightly different way to our ancestors. The world is a different place. Although we still create sacred space, commune with nature and the Goddess, and do our Grove workings in a circle, we try to leave no trace of where we have been. We still visit stone circles and groves of trees like our Celtic ancestors, but we tend to make use of what is already there, connecting and working with the spirit of a place as it already exists.

Preparation

Before you begin to think about casting a circle for your working, you need to prepare yourself and a few items. As an example, we will discuss casting a circle for a solo Druid to do a working. You do not always need to cast a circle. Certain rituals and most meditations do not require it. Indeed, there are times when the casting of a circle is entirely inappropriate.

To begin with, you need to consider the location of your circle. This depends, in part, on the number of people involved. Some Druids occasionally work in large, open Gorseddau. These are meetings of Druids from several or many Orders and Groves, generally (though not always) held in public places. The Druid presiding over the ceremony will generally walk the circle outside of those attending, casting as they go. Other Druids work just with the Grove they belong to or on their own.

Outdoors is the ideal place. We call upon the spirits of the natural world to aid us in our work and it is simple politeness to meet them on their home ground. They are far more likely to respond. However, circumstances can dictate against working outside and it is very much up to the individuals involved to decide which location is best at a given time.

That said, for our walk-through we will use a room indoors. When you are beginning, you need to be able to concentrate on what you are doing. Choose familiar surroundings in which you know you will not be disturbed by people, the elements, or curious creatures. Once you know the content of the ritual, you can take it outside and apply it to a more open environment.

Decide what room you will use. You will need space to walk around a small circle as well as room to sit in the centre. Try to have this room uncluttered, as well as clean and tidy. Preparing the site of any ritual is as important as the ritual itself and helps you achieve the correct frame of mind for the work you are about to undertake.

If you decide on candles – which provide a kinder and subtler form of illumination than electric light - do be careful of where you place them. Keep them well away from curtains and fabrics. And remember that you will be moving around (perhaps in robes) which can cause drafts. Sturdy candleholders with wide bases (for stability and to catch running wax) are highly recommended.

Decide what you will need in the centre of your circle. You might want nothing. Alternatively, you might like a cushion to sit on, a central flame (candle), a stone you are fond of, some flowers, anything you wish that is appropriate to the ritual or working you are about to undertake. For the example that follows, you will need a small bowl of water, some incense (either loose or a stick) and matches, and your athame or wand. Put all of these items in the room before you start.

You next need to work out where north is, so you can accurately call the quarters. A compass is always useful to have (especially when you start working outside), but if you know, for example, that the window faces north, that will do. If you are using loose incense, light the charcoal in advance of the ritual as it takes a while to get hot enough.

How it is done, step by step.
Turn off the phone. You will be amazed at how many people decide to call you the minute you sit down to work or meditate. Ask anyone else in the house not to disturb you until you have finished (unless, of course, the place is on fire). This is very important. You will not be harmed if you are disturbed, but you cannot work properly unless you are confident that others are respecting your space.

A bath is a good way to prepare for your Druid work. A symbolic cleansing, using scented oils, is an excellent way to focus your thoughts and attain an appropriate state of mind in readiness for entering your sacred space. You can then put on your robes (if you use them) and go straight through to the room that you have prepared.

When you are ready, move the water to the west of centre on the floor, and the incense to the south, again on the floor. You then need to walk deiseal (sunwise or clockwise) around to the gateway at the west (do not forget your wand or athame if using one) and stand there for a moment, facing east.

All your movements should be deiseal, even when turning on the spot. This keeps the energies flowing in the same direction. To walk the circle anticlockwise is known as going tuathal, and it is for taking down energies and banishing, especially at the end of rituals. We do not want to banish energies just yet, so keep everything flowing the same way.

You will not come to any harm if you walk in the wrong direction; it simply dilutes your hard work and disperses the flow. Try to get into the habit of doing everything deiseal, even stirring drinks.

As you stand in the west, facing the east, you are on the threshold of what will be your circle. Wait until you feel it is right to enter. When you first start to cast circles, it is difficult to believe you will feel this, but there will be a definite moment when you know all is ready.

Walk through the gateway and move deiseal around to the opposite side, the east. Face outwards and give a salute to the spirit of the east, the Guardians of the circle, the spirits of place. How you salute them is up to you. Some raise one hand, whilst others hold up both arms. Some simply make contact. This salutation is best done with your eyes closed.

If you are working alone, walk the complete circle again, finishing back in the east. Turn to face inwards. You then make a statement of intent, whilst asking for guidance from the Goddess. This tells the spirits of place why you are there so they may respond appropriately. After this is done, turn and face the south. You are now ready to cast the circle.

Take your wand or athame in your right hand (if you are using your finger, it is still the right hand). This is not 'handist'. Apart from anything else, the Druid Way is a Sun path. If you face the rising Sun in the northern hemisphere (where the Druid Way originated), it moves to your right. Working with the right hand to set up sacred space is symbolic of this path.

Hold your arm out straight across your body and below shoulder height so that you make the circle outside of you as you walk. Visualize energy coming up from the Earth and down from the Stars, meeting within you and travelling along your arm into the wand, athame, or finger.

Start to walk slowly round from east to east, the path of the Sun. As you do so, feel and see the energy flowing from your arm, forming a circle of light. When you return to the east, and the circle of light is complete, turn and face the centre.

You will now consecrate the circle with fire and water. It must be pointed out here that some traditions (particularly within witchcraft) use salted water. Do not use this outside as salt can kill plants and the small creatures that live in the soil.

From the east, walk the circle to the south, pick up the incense holder, and walk from south to south with it. Place it in the centre. Walk to the west, pick up the water, and walk from west to west. You can sprinkle some water around the circle as you go if you wish.

These two acts consecrate and secure the circle. You are now in protective space. Whatever you do inside the circle will stay there until you disperse it, use it (as in a healing ritual), or close everything down. Undesirable influences will not penetrate it while you work. You have created a centre to your own universe.

When you have put the water in the centre, step straight back, and then walk round to the east. You will now give peace to the quarters, something that is done in most Druid circles worldwide. You move to each of the cardinal points, starting in the north and then moving to the south, west, and east. It may seem an odd order, but the quarters are worked as opposites so that the energies running between them establish a central point within the circle.

In many Druid rituals, a prayer is now said. This is a supplication for those gifts and qualities we most associate with being Druid. Next, come the invocations. These are to invite those from other planes that you would like to enter your circle. Normally it is the Goddess and God, but it could also be a particular deity such as Brigid for an Imbolc or healing ritual. Invocations do not need to be complicated. Simply ask politely for the presence of those that you wish to be in your circle.

A word of warning here. Be very sure of who or what you are inviting in, and why you want them to be there. If it is a deity, make sure you know their history. Some are difficult to work with. All bring particular energies that should be appropriate to the occasion.

It is also important that you do not mix rays. If, for example, you invite the Dagda into your circle, remember he is Irish and teaming him up with Isis, who is Egyptian, just will not work. Stay with the Celtic pantheon, which is enormous, but also do your research, as even within this there are deities and spirits whose energies will clash.

The same warning goes for inviting faerie folk. This has become something of a fashion and it sounds wonderful, but not all faeries are friendly and they can be very hard to get rid of afterwards. Celtic faeries are not the pretty little flimsies with wings that we see in picture books any more than they are elementals or elves.

Following the invocations, you will open the gateways at the four quarters (which we give capital letters to differentiate them from the cardinal points). This allows power and energy from each of the quarters to enter your circle; it also gives added protection. Starting with the East, the place of air, the dawn, birds, and spring, you do what is known as 'calling the quarter'. You then move around deiseal to the south, west, and north, before returning to the east. Calling the quarters is done facing outwards.

When you get back to the east, you turn to face the centre and declare the completion of the circle and the opening of the ritual. You may now do your central working. This could be a meditation, an Inner Grove working, a ritual celebration, a healing, anything at all to do with your Druid work.

When you have finished the central section, it is very important that the circle be closed down properly. No trace should be left on any plane of existence, physical or astral. Time and space should be allowed to return as they were before. All gateways to the quarters must be closed. All visitors to your circle must depart back to their own worlds. This is known as the 'closing'.

You should start this process by stating that the ritual has ended and that you have finished your work. The Oath of Peace is often said three times, followed by the Awen. This is intoned or chanted as many times as you wish, normally in multiples of three.

You will then need to thank the four quarters for their help and let them depart. This begins with the North, and then moves to the West, South, and East. You still walk deiseal at this point. If there is a Druid in each quarter, they would each face outwards and close the gateways in turn, but working solo, you need to walk around.

When you have visualized the gateways closing, turn inwards and thank all those who have come to your circle, seen and unseen, and ask them politely to leave. Try not to forget anyone. Then, finally, declare that the ritual has finished.

Take up your wand or athame, or using your finger, walk from east to east. This time walk tuathal just inside the circle that you cast, seeing the light draw back into your wand, athame, or finger, down your body into the Earth and back up to the Stars.

Turn to face the east and salute it, before walking deiseal to the place of the ancestors, the west. This is your gateway by which to leave. When you feel ready, step out, and know that you have returned to this world. Quietly clear your things away and finish with a drink and something to eat which helps to ground you in this reality.

Try to avoid leaving a circle during a working. If it becomes necessary, go to the west and cut a doorway (psychically) tuathal, step through, and turn to face the circle. Close the doorway by pulling the circle back deiseal so it joins. When you go back in do the same, but walk a complete circle deiseal when you re-enter to get the energies flowing again.

This all seems very long and difficult to begin with. We hope that by explaining it, you have come to understand the structure and the reasons why you do certain things. This in turn should make the whole thing easier to remember. In addition, the more you perform such rituals, the easier they become, leaving you free to concentrate on the working within.

No harm will come to you if you make mistakes, as there is no real right or wrong way to do things as you travel the Druid Way. The Goddess does not expect us to be perfect beings and no one is watching in judgement over you. It is the intention behind your workings that is important, hence the need to become conversant with the Celtic metaphysic. Having said that, the form of the rituals presented herein is important. They are tried and tested ways in which to protect yourself and to raise energy.

Most of the rituals in this book have been written for the solo or Hedge Druid. Some, however, require more participants where witness to an event is required. The openings and closings for both solo work and for groups can be applied to all the appropriate rituals. They are given separately, following this chapter. Thereafter, only the central working of each ritual is given, except for the Binding rite, which is slightly different. Actions are given in an italic typeface; spoken parts are in normal typeface.

We have kept the rituals themselves as simple as possible. This is because we believe it allows you to concentrate on the meaning, rather than worrying about cumbersome or archaic language, complex movements, and large amounts of paraphernalia.

Furthermore, it is important to remember that the rituals herein are not set in stone. They were written as a guide for those new to the Druid Way. They were written so that those new to the Way could participate fully in being Druid from their very first step.

Once you have become familiar with them and the reason why they are the shape they are, please feel free to adapt them to suit your own needs and circumstance. To begin with, this may simply be to accommodate their use with small groups or Groves.

As your understanding evolves and your personal path develops, you may want to change the symbology and deities to better reflect your vision of the eightfold year, your rites of passage, and the greater mysteries of being. Or perhaps you feel unhappy with working with specific deities. In which case, you can simply call on the Goddess and the God. They know what aspect of their self accords with your work.

Remember, however, that the rituals were conceived and developed as a balanced whole. If you alter one aspect, you will need to consider how that affects all the others. This will require research, meditation, and familiarity with the rituals based in experience.

Working with and developing the rituals in this way is an act of empowerment. Not only does it make each ritual a living entity, it makes it an extension of your own being. Rituals are, after all, a great deal more than poetry recited by candlelight.

With one or two obvious exceptions (birth, house blessing, and death), the rituals can and should, wherever possible, be performed outdoors. We are, after all, Druids and it is from the natural world that we derive our strength, knowledge, understanding, wisdom, and enlightenment. It is with the natural world that we work to unify ourselves.

There are, of course, always exceptions. We are human and the weather can sometimes be atrocious. However, if you feel it necessary to hold your ritual indoors to prevent the onset of pneumonia or frostbite, try to make some observance outside as well on the day, even if it is only a brief invocation to petition for the success of the forthcoming ceremony. Try also to go outside directly you have finished to make contact with the Land. Take what the ritual has given you, along with any offerings of bread and mead, and pass these on as gifts. What is given to you can be shared without diminishing its worth.

There is another reason we have kept the rituals simple - so that everyone can participate. Druids, like all other material beings, come with bits that do not work. For many, stomping several miles through wild woodland with bagfuls of paraphernalia to perform a prolonged and complicated ritual is out of the question. In fact, it actively discriminates against the disabled.

For those who cannot get outside, there is no shame in this. Our ancestors treated their sick and disabled with a great deal of respect and compassion. Hospitals, physicians, and nourishing food were all supplied - along with compensation for injuries caused by others. Moreover, in common with many other cultures, ancestral Celts recognized that what we call physical or mental disability was a gift that could set those so 'afflicted' several steps ahead of everyone else in the quest for spiritual understanding and enlightenment.

Whatever your circumstance, there is one thing to which you must pay particular attention - fire. Whilst it no doubt adds enormously to the ambience of any ritual, it can be extremely dangerous if not properly cared for. If you are working alone, whether indoors or out, use a nightlight in a lantern and make sure it is secure. If you are working in a group, especially when you are outdoors, appoint someone as a fire monitor even if you only have a single lantern. Bonfires are not particularly environmentally friendly, but if you do have one it will be the monitor's task to ensure safety, including being certain that any fire is fully doused before you leave the site of your ritual. This is far more important than closing the circle as you can always go back and close down spiritual energies. Once fire has escaped, it is out for good - or bad.

General preparations for ritual working, along with the casting of a circle in which to work, are to be found with the openings and closings. Before you attempt any ritual, read the opening, central section, and closing through several times in full. Not only will you know what is needed and where it must be placed before the ritual begins, but it also gives you a feel for the ritual. Eventually you will come to know them by heart and will be able to perform them wherever you happen to be.

SOLO RITUALS - OPENING AND CLOSING

For this solo opening and closing you will require incense, a burner, matches or a lighter, and water in a bowl. Set everything out beforehand, along with anything you may need for the central working.

Opening
Enter from the west and walk deiseal to salute the east. Walk a circuit back to the east and turn outwards.

Oh, Great Goddess, I ask for your blessing, guidance, and protection on this my ritual for [*name of ceremony*].

Cast your circle from east to east. Walk to the south and take the incense round the circle. Walk to the west and do the same with the water. Return to the east. Walk to the north and turn outwards. As you salute the quarter, say:

May there be peace in the North.

Walk to the south and turn outwards. As you salute the quarter, say:

May there be peace in the South.

Walk to the west and turn outwards. As you salute the quarter, say:

May there be peace in the West.

Walk to the east and turn outwards. As you salute the quarter, say:

May there be peace in the East.

Turn to face the centre. Say:

May there be peace above and peace below. May there be peace throughout the worlds.

Say the prayer:

May I be blessed with the cauldron's gift,
May the breath of inspiration touch me,
May my voice always sing clear,
May the light reach within me,
May I learn from the Land,
May the seeds I plant be fruit for all children,
May calm be my mantle,
May wisdom blaze out from the depths of my soul,
May truth be in my heart.

Say the Invocations:

O Great Goddess,
Bringer of life,
Queen of the Stars,
Mother of the Earth and Seas,
Be present now within this place.

O Great God,
Lord of the Land,
Guardian of the Wild Wood,
Walker of the silent ways,
Be present now within this place.

Turn outwards and say:

In the name of the spirit of Hawk, the springtime breeze, and the element of Air, I open this eastern gateway.

Walk to the south. Turn outwards and say:

In the name of the spirit of Adder, the power of the Sun, and the element of Fire, I open this southern gateway.

Walk to the west. Turn outwards and say:

In the name of the spirit of the Sacred Salmon, mighty oceans, and the element of Water, I open this western gateway.

Walk to the north. Turn outwards and say:

In the name of the spirit of Wolf, of dark, deep forests, and the element of Earth, I open this northern gateway.

Walk to the east. Turn inwards and say:

This circle is complete. In this sacred place, I declare the opening of this my ritual for [*name of ceremony*].

Central working

Closing
When you have completed your central working, say:

I declare that my work is done within this circle this day. May my memory and my heart hold its sacredness.

Swear the Oath of Peace three times.

I swear by peace and love to stand, heart to heart and hand in hand, mark O spirit and hear me now, confirming this my sacred vow.

Intone the Awen as many times as you like.

Walk to the north. Turn outwards and say:

Spirits of the midnight cold, of crystal, and stone, I thank the element of Earth and close this northern gateway.

Walk to the west. Turn outwards and say:

Spirits of evening light, of sacred spring and well, I thank the element of Water and close this western gateway.

Walk to the south. Turn outwards and say:

Spirits of the Sun at noon, of mighty oak, and the sacred flame, I thank the element of Fire and close this southern gateway.

Walk to the east. Turn outwards and say:

Spirits of the dawn, of lofty hill, and mighty gales, I thank the element of Air and close this eastern gateway.

Face the centre and say:

I thank the Goddess and the God, and all those seen and unseen who have joined this circle today.

Depart in peace. Hail and Farewell.

I send healing and love to the animal, plant, and mineral kingdoms. May they always be protected from harm.

I declare this ritual for [*name of ceremony*] is now ended. It ends in peace, as in peace it began.

Close your circle tuathal, grounding it back into the Earth and up to the Stars. When you reach the east again, turn outwards and salute it, before walking deiseal to the west and leaving.

GROUP RITUAL - OPENING AND CLOSING

For this group opening and closing you will require incense, a burner, matches or a lighter, and water in a bowl. Set everything out beforehand, along with anything you may need for the central working.

The way in which you allocate and organize the calling of the quarters will depend, of course, on how many people there are in the group. It may be easier to nominate one person to open and close whilst others conduct the central working. Remember to sort out the order in which you need to enter the circle so that each person reaches their correct position straight away.

Opening
All enter from the west and walk deiseal. As each person reaches the east, they turn outward to salute the quarter and then continue walking around the circle until they reach their allotted station.

East: Oh, Great Goddess, we ask for your blessing, guidance, and protection on this our ritual for [*name of ceremony*].

East casts the circle deiseal from east back to east.

South: (*Walks round the circle with incense.*) I bless and consecrate this circle with fire.

West: (*Walks round the circle with water.*) I bless and consecrate this circle with water.

East: Let us now send peace to the quarters.

North: (*Turns outwards and salutes.*) May there be peace in the North.

South: (*Turns outwards and salutes.*) May there be peace in the South.

West: (*Turns outwards and salutes.*) May there be peace in the West.

East: (*Turns outwards and salutes.*) May there be peace in the East.

All: (*Face inwards.*) May there be peace above and peace below. May there be peace throughout the worlds.

After a suitable pause, all continue with the prayer:

May we be blessed with the cauldron's gift,
May the breath of inspiration touch us,
May our voices always sing,
May the light reach within us,
May we learn from the Land,
May the seeds we plant be fruit for all children,
May calm be our mantle,
May wisdom blaze out from the depths of our souls,
May truth be in our hearts.

West: O Great Goddess,
Bringer of life,
Queen of the Stars,
Mother of the Earth and Seas,
Be present now within this place.

South: O Great God,
Lord of the Land,
Guardian of the Wild Wood,
Walker of the silent ways,
Be present now within this place.

East: Let the four directions be honoured within our circle. (*Turns outwards.*) In the name of the spirit of Hawk, the springtime breeze, and the element of Air, I open this eastern gateway.

South: (*Turns outwards.*) In the name of the spirit of Adder, the power of the Sun, and the element of Fire, I open this southern gateway.

West: (*Turns outwards.*) In the name of the spirit of the Sacred Salmon, mighty oceans, and the element of Water, I open this western gateway.

North: (*Turns outwards.*) In the name of the spirit of Wolf, of dark, deep forests, and the element of Earth, I open this northern gateway.

All turn towards the centre.

East: Our circle is complete. We have created sacred space. I declare the opening of this ritual for [*name of ceremony*].

Central working

Closing
When your central working is complete, close as follows.

East: We declare that our work is done within this circle this day. May our memories and our hearts hold its sacredness.

All hold hands in a circle to swear the Oath of Peace three times.

All: We swear by peace and love to stand, heart to heart and hand in hand, mark O spirit and hear us now, confirming this our sacred vow.

All intone the Awen as many times as you like.

North: (*Turns outwards.*) Spirits of the midnight cold, of crystal, and stone, I thank the element of Earth and close this northern gateway.

West: (*Turns outwards.*) Spirits of evening light, of sacred spring and well, I thank the element of Water and close this western gateway.

South: (*Turns outwards.*) Spirits of the Sun at noon, of mighty oak, and the sacred flame, I thank the element of Fire and close this southern gateway.

East: (*Turns outwards.*) Spirits of the dawn, of lofty hill, and mighty gales, I thank the element of Air and close this eastern gateway.

All turn to face the centre.

North: We thank the Goddess and the God, and all those seen and unseen who have joined our circle this day. Depart in peace. Hail and Farewell.

West: We send healing and love to the animal, plant, and mineral kingdoms. May they always be protected from harm.

East: I declare this ritual for [*name of ceremony*] is now ended. It closes in peace, as in peace it began.

East closes the circle tuathal, grounding it back into the Earth and up to the Stars. Everyone walks the circle again, each turning outward at the east to salute the quarter before continuing to the west and leaving.

PART ONE

THE SKY

THE EIGHTFOLD YEAR

Of all the rituals associated with Druids, it is those that mark out the turning of the year that first spring to mind. As they are celebrations of the shape of the year and the movements of the Sun and the Moon determine their timing, we have called them Sky rituals.

This is not an absolute demarcation, but a matter of emphasis. Although we also have distinct Land rituals and Sea rituals (so representing the elements of Celtic tradition), all three elements are present in each.

Some detail of these aspects and their meaning is discussed with each ritual below. For the moment, we will confine ourselves to considering an overview of the pattern made by these ceremonies during the annual cycle.

It is important, from the outset, to remember that what we are celebrating is a cycle. Linear thought and application belongs to the modern scientific metaphysic that currently dominates most people's thinking. Yet purely linear features are rare beyond modern human thought and construction (and then mostly to be found within the mineral kingdom). Even the most cursory study of the world about us reveals that everything unfolds and evolves in a cyclical fashion.

The most obvious examples of this are the diurnal cycle of light and dark, the lunar cycle, and the changing of the seasons as sunrise and sunset travel back and forth along the eastern and western horizons. These particular cycles are caused by the movement of the Earth and Moon about each other and the journey of both about the Sun.

The rhythms created by this cosmic dance are a major influence on our lives and govern much of our behaviour. After all, we evolved as a species over millions of years with these cycles as constant and important companions. There are minor regional variations, but the overall effect is the same and they have shaped us at a fundamental level.

Even in highly industrialized societies, these cycles cannot be ignored, albeit that many people simply look on them as inconveniences. If they took greater note of them and learned to live their lives properly in tune with them (instead of trying to cheat them) these people would be healthier and happier.

It is no accident, therefore, that many different peoples have celebrated the significant stages in the cycles of the Sun and the Moon and formalized their celebration with ritual. Woven in with this reverence for what has helped to shape us are the many mythologies that help connect the abstract concepts with the everyday - reflecting people's experience of these events.

Before we go any further, just a quick note on terminology. The reason for calling the solar festivals 'solar' is obvious as they mark the passage of the sun in relation to the horizon and thus delineate the cycle of the year (the period in which the earth moves once around the sun).

To mark out the other ceremonies in contrast, we will refer to them throughout as lunar festivals. This is a convenience. As we shall see, there is a great deal more to it than this, and using the term 'lunar' has much more to do with symbolism than it does with using the Moon to gauge when the ceremonies should be held. And whilst everyone celebrated the event at hand, there was a deeper recognition of the aspects involved in this communion with the way in which the universe worked. The lunar and solar cycles wove together as part of a greater unity and this, too, was celebrated.

When it comes to the dance of Sun, Earth, and Moon, there are eight festivals in all, celebrated every six weeks or so. In terms of Celtic tradition, there is a degree of controversy over the eightfold year. Four of the festivals are well attested and some have even survived to the present day - still celebrated in some form or other in various parts of the UK. These are the four lunar festivals - Imbolc, Beltane, Lughnasad, and Samhain. They are sometimes also referred to as the fire festivals and they delineate the seasons and celebrate the agricultural cycle.

Some have questioned the legitimacy of the four festivals that fall between these, the solar festivals that mark the solstices and equinoxes. However, they are genuinely Celtic and were observed by Druids and ordinary folk alike. Indeed, it is inconceivable that a people with so many solar deities in their pantheon would not celebrate the cycle of the Sun.

In fact, the solar ceremonies appear more in surviving literature than the lunar festivals. It is just that they are not overtly mentioned. Their obscurity is not such that it could be argued there is a bending of the truth. Simply that when a festival is part of your everyday culture, you do not go out of your way to explain it. And whereas the lunar ceremonies have survived by dint of being subsumed into folk culture as festivals marking the seasons, the solar ceremonies (which were quiet celebrations of the inner mysteries) faded with the passing of the power of the Druids - where, that is, they were not subsumed by Christianity.

However much the celebrations of the solar cycle may have faded, the stories and myths associated with it took on a life of their own, developing into an unparalleled canon of mystical literature over the centuries - the Matter of Britain.

If we look in Arthurian literature and its associated tales, we find that key moments of these stories occur at the solstices and equinoxes. That these dates have later been Christianized does not disguise their clear pre-Christian origin (any more than it disguises the fact that Christians felt the need to subsume such powerful events into their own mythology). Nor should we be confounded by those who tell us that certain aspects of the Matter of Britain (for example, the Round Table) were late additions. That they are mentioned first in later texts does not mean they do not have their origin in the pagan solar mythology.

The clearest examples of all this can be found in events linked with the winter solstice - the most important single text in this respect being *Sir Gawain and the Green Knight*. Although written in the fourteenth century, many aspects of this exceptional poem speak of a much earlier origin. The characters and symbolism are clearly pre-Christian. Gawain is a solar figure. His strength waxes and wanes with the Sun's passage across the sky, being greatest at midsummer and reaching a peak each midday. The device on his shield is a pentangle that, although given a Christian gloss, is clearly a powerful pagan symbol – not least, because it is an endless knot representing the cyclical nature of things.

In early texts, Gawain follows adventures that parallel those of the Mabon, the divine child who is reborn each winter solstice. In *Sir Gawain and the Green Knight*, he champions Arthur, the Sun King, when a mysterious green man carrying a great bundle of holly proposes a beheading game at the winter solstice feast. Making the first blow, Gawain strikes the head from the green man – who then retrieves his severed pate and summons Gawain to his castle to receive the return blow at the next winter solstice.

Gawain seeks out the green man. His courage, morals, and instinctive wisdom, along with his strength (even at its weakest), allow him to win through. Although not explicitly stated in the poem, this brings about the regeneration of the kingdom of Arthur which otherwise would have been brought into disrepute and faced the destruction of perpetual winter.

The tale is about duty and self-sacrifice, about keeping faith. It is about service and rebirth. The story begins and ends on the winter solstice (Christianized to New Year and Christmas-tide) and Gawain sets out on his quest to find the Green Knight on Samhain. There are many other pointers to the importance of the winter solstice and the rituals, deities, and symbols connected with it in the text.

Yet that is not the only tale that points to the celebration of the winter solstice or its supreme importance. Even within the Matter of Britain, it becomes clear that the day of shortest light is of supreme importance to pagan Britons. Both Uther and Arthur decreed it to be a major feast day. Both held court at this time.

Most importantly, however, was that Arthur was first revealed to the world by drawing the sword from the stone on the winter solstice. This supremely nascent act at the turning point of the year is replete with symbolism of all kinds. It marks the beginning of new life and new hope, of the beginning of a process that will lead to the healing of the wasteland and the integration of a spiritual realm with its material counterpart. It is why so many ancestral ceremonial and sacred sites are aligned with midwinter sunrise. It is why both authors of this work consider this to be *the* most important of the eight ceremonies that mark the turning of the year.

But what of the other solar festivals? The next in sequence is the spring equinox. This was subsumed into the Christian ceremony of Easter – the date of which is determined by the lunar and solar cycles. In the later tales, this became the highest feast day of the year, although it is clear that this change in emphasis is probably due to Christian redactors. Uther did not decree it to be a feast day. That Arthur did, is used by some to state that Arthur was a Christian king. It is unlikely that the historical Arthur was ever a king in any formal sense and early hagiography paints him as a ravager of the Church - not very Christian at all.

What is more likely is that the spring equinox was reinstated as an important festival during the Arthurian period. The removal of the formal Roman protection of Britain saw a re-establishment of

Celtic identity. Many of the old customs found new life or, at least, were practised more openly. The most important events in the Matter of Britain that occur at this time certainly have a pagan feel about them.

Uther was crowned at the spring equinox and he met Ygerne. These events are not unconnected (it is, after all, a period of fertility) and they are far more complex than the Christianized version of these events would suggest. Uther was not a lustful bully who went to war simply to have sex with another man's wife. Ygerne is an embodiment of the Goddess and the conflict between Uther and Gorlois personifies the age-old change of the champions of Sovereignty. The result of this union, brought about with the aid of Myrddin, was Arthur himself - who was to become the supreme champion and consort of the Goddess.

The other major events attached to the spring equinox concern the Grail. That the Grail cycle has its roots in pre-Christian religion is beyond doubt. The nature of the Grail, and the unravelling of the quest to find it have been much adapted over the centuries and it speaks volumes that the symbolism of the stories is still extremely potent.

At the spring equinox, the Grail (a vessel of renewal, the fertile egg, the newly gravid woman) was itself recharged. This marks the transition from the uncertainties of early spring when the first buds and the first-born are still vulnerable to late frosts and chilling rains, to the certainty of days longer than nights, of growing warmth and strength, of the coming of summer, of potential fully realized.

The summer solstice (often given as Midsummer's Day or St John's Day) is marked with a plethora of events, many connected with fire and victory in battle. The sun is at its greatest strength and has won through to provide peace and plenty. This parallels the life of Arthur and presages what is to follow, for each year as the sun reaches the peak of its power, it inevitably begins to lose that power and influence. This is echoed in the meeting between the Mabon and Arthur, the introduction of the Lancelot of the Lake to the court, and the meeting between Myrddin and the Lady of the Lake - all of which occur at the summer solstice. These are all people in their prime and these are all people involved in events that mark the beginning of their inevitable and natural decline.

This is seen by many as great tragedy, not least because of the way in which the tales were later retold (largely by those who did not understand or who wished to traduce the pagan metaphysic on which they are based). In human terms, these are indeed tragedies, because the downfall of the characters is inevitable. However, to leave it at that is to take a linear view of things.

Arthur cannot remain as champion of the Goddess forever. Myrddin cannot always be there to guide him. Everyone, once they reach their prime, is also at the beginning of their decline. They will grow old, their influence will fade, daylight hours will shorten, and they will all, eventually, die. But in the cycle of being, there comes a point when strength can fade no more, when days are at their shortest, nights at their longest and the Winter King reaches his own strongest point - only to see his powers diminish as a new Mabon is born.

Arthurian material is scant when it comes to the autumn equinox. This is not so much due to a lack of events, but to the fact that many of them have been moved and take place at Samhain (All Hallow's Eve), even though they are entirely inappropriate at that juncture. As we see from Hallowe'en's manufactured emphasis on ghouls and ghosts, the nature of the festival has been changed so that the emphasis is on death. Samhain, however, is a ceremony of remembrance and of converse with the ancestors – a festival of those who have new life in the Otherworld. It is the autumn equinox, the point after which nights become longer than days, that marks death in its widest sense.

The still moment of equinox between summer and winter is when the power of the Grail truly re-asserts itself. Characters associated with the Grail come to the fore and the quest itself is attained - ensuring that winter will be but temporary and that the waste land will be restored to fertility after a necessary period of rest. Thus it is that Peredur attains his goal and is crowned Fisher King - that is to say, King of the Water, King of the Otherworld, provider for his people.

This is his service, his sacrifice, his death. To attain the Grail - the means of generation and regeneration - and to channel its vital energies is to give up one's own material existence. Ultimately, the Grail is not of this world, even though it manifests here. It is an idea, a way of living and of viewing the world that is at odds with the ever-increasing destructiveness of so-called civilized life. To seek the Grail is to turn away from that and live more lightly. To be one with the Grail, to enter ultimate service in its name, is to commit one's self wholly to the Otherworld.

In a less exalted sense, the equinox also marks the point at which we must commit ourselves to the winter. In ancestral times this was a matter of harvesting, preparing the fields for spring sowing, ensuring a plentiful supply of firewood and preserved food, and generally withdrawing to the confines of the homestead and the hearth. Today we are more likely to begin tidying our gardens and thinking about all those indoor tasks that need to be done.

There are many other reasons for supposing that there were eight ceremonies in a year, not least the fact that major events in the Arthurian tales can also be found on the four lunar festivals. Moreover, the Matter of Britain is far from being the sole source of information on this. As we have mentioned, the two major ways of measuring time made use of the Sun and the Moon as markers. The day, the month, and the year, owe their existence to the complex dance of the Earth and the Moon about the Sun. Each body had its associated deities, and each of these would have been celebrated at points appropriate to the dance.

The solar and lunar were, thus, interwoven to reflect the complex and holistic nature of being. The lunar festivals were governed by the agricultural existence of our ancestors and had to reflect their daily life and experience. Celebration was woven in with practical concerns. The need to meet, exchange goods and news, perform ceremonies in the public eye, conclude deals and settle disputes, and ask the gods and goddesses for continued protection was as much an occasion for song, dance, gossip, and a drink as it was for solemnity. Truth and joy are good companions.

That all this was presided over by Druids is without question. Their position within Celtic society would have demanded it. However, they were not just there in their official capacity. Druids were and are just as likely to want to celebrate the material, be it a good harvest or the treasured memory of loved ones now on their long journey to the Summerlands.

The solar ceremonies were a counterbalance to this. For all that they were probably held in broad daylight, they celebrated the spiritual cycle of the year and of life. In all likelihood, they were quiet, formal occasions creating a mystical atmosphere in which people could reflect on and give thanks for their relationship with the spiritual domain. Perhaps, too, Druids had private ceremonies when they could reflect on their own being rather than ministering to others.

Although the content of these ceremonies may have been lost to us, the intent is still apparent. Christmas and Easter, for example, may have become heavily commercialized, but many people still recognize in some confused way that these are times of the spirit. On the other hand, we still light fires at Samhain and have parties, albeit we now call it Bonfire Night.

The solar festivals are absolute within the year, as those four days define the year (even if the Gregorian calendar moves a day or two back and forth about them). The lunar festivals are much more problematical. We know the Celtic lunar calendar was sophisticated, but any system that tries to meld lunar and solar cycles will only coincide every nineteen years (and then not exactly, as they are several hours out of synchronization).

The months (running from full moon to full moon) drifted back and forth in relation to the solar cycle that was the fixed framework. Festivals could not be standardized to the first day of certain months. The movement of the months would mean that a ceremony to celebrate the bringing in of the harvest could be held weeks before the crops were even ripe. We have become too used to a solar calendar to appreciate this.

To confuse this further, there is some evidence to suggest that each of the four lunar festivals was each celebrated in relation to a different phase of the moon. Samhain was connected with the dark moon, Imbolc with the first quarter, and so on. Calculating this in conjunction with the nineteen years drift of the months was one of the tasks of the Druid to ensure that each festival fell at the appropriate time.

If you have the freedom to do this, then by all means do so. The basic calculations are simple. Lunar festivals fall approximately 45 days after solar festivals. The correct quarter of the moon nearest that can then be ascertained and the date for the lunar festival set. This is made all the easier if you get into the habit of following the lunar cycle.

However, we live in the twenty-first century and there are many pressures on us that our ancestors did not face. We are tied by many considerations to a solar calendar. We can, of course, work out the exact date of festivals in advance and book our holidays accordingly, but this can be pedantic to the point of missing the point.

Our Celtic ancestors were a fluid people who knew that the observance of the cycle was more important than making sure it was done at precisely the correct time. Most present-day Druids celebrate the eightfold year on the conventional dates (and very often on the weekend nearest those). Others perform quiet private rituals at the correct time and more open ceremonies at the nearest convenient date. Do not worry about this. Whilst we would encourage you to be as accurate as possible and be aware of the movements and cycles of both Sun and Moon, we would reiterate that an understanding of the cycle and the keeping of it in spirit is much more important and effective than soulless pedantry. These are, after all is said and done, celebrations.

IMBOLC

Imbolc is the ceremony with which we celebrate the promise of spring. Although the days are still cold and wet, they are now becoming perceptibly longer - final proof that the Sun-child reborn at the winter solstice has survived and thrives. The year is quickening and you will see the first signs of life returning to the Land. The Sun itself now has sufficient strength to warm the soil. Snowdrops may well be in flower. Lambs can be seen in the fields and byres, and the ewes are in milk. The whiteness of snow and frost is replaced by the lightness of warmth and new life.

It was traditional in some areas at this time to plait a cross within a circle from wheat straw to decorate the hearth. This symbol, better known as a Sun cross or Celtic cross was made from pieces of straw specially preserved from the previous harvest. It was the Sun that had ripened the straw, and using it to make a solar symbol was one way in which the Sun was both honoured and invoked.

The essential feature of Imbolc, however, is the honouring of the Goddess, of Woman, of the Land - all imbued with the power and the responsibility of bringing forth life. This ultimate and essential act of creativity is celebrated in verse and song and is personified by the Goddess Brigid (pronounced approximately as 'breed' and meaning 'the exalted one' or 'the sublime one'). She is, in common with many Celtic deities, triple-aspected; a goddess of healing and fertility, a goddess of smiths, and a goddess of poetry - all of which are associated with fire and flame, with the hearth, with creativity.

Brigid is a daughter of The Dagda and often appears wearing a crown of light. A perpetual flame was kept in her honour in a sacred grove at what is now known as Kildare (which means 'church of the oaks'). This was a female enclave, not uncommon in ancestral times, and was a centre of learning for medicine, the bardic arts and, quite possibly, the martial arts.

Although this is a time to celebrate the promise of spring, it is also a reminder that it is just that - a promise. Nothing is certain during the early steps on any journey. It is, therefore, also a time to be wary, a time to call on our reserves of strength. Our ancestors knew this only too well. By this stage of the year, they had survived the winter on what they could store away and although the Sun was gathering strength, their own supplies would be getting low. The new growth and early vegetables could still be blighted by late frosts.

At this time of renewed vigilance, Brigid's gifts are most appropriate. Life in its early stages is always precarious, be it for the lamb, the human child, the seedling, or the community. And so it is for the spirit. There comes that stage in the journey when our first reserves of enthusiasm for what is new have worn low and we see before us the length of the journey. Just as many people feel that winter will never end, so many on the spiritual path despair that they will ever understand, that the goal they have set themselves can be won. Brigid can heal, Brigid can sing a charm, and Brigid can arm us all at the forge for whatever battles we may face.

So important was Brigid to the Celtic peoples that her cult was almost wholly subsumed into Christianity. It was an historical figure by the name of Brigit, who was born in AD 450 and died in AD 523, who became known as St Brigit. Her feast day is, of course, 1 February, followed by Candlemass on 2 February when her crown of light was replicated in churches by the lighting of candles.

As an Irish saint, she is second only to St Patrick in common popularity. After her death, many of the stories and attributes of Brigid were attached to written accounts of her life. Yet even the single act of her life that is accepted by the Christian Church - that she founded a nunnery at Kildare - is highly doubtful. Some have argued, from reasonably strong evidence, that the historical Brigit was a Druidess who converted to Christianity (or held to both faiths as many Druids did at this time). In most accounts of her life, her father is given as a Druid called Dubhthach.

Preparation

Although warmth is returning to the world, the emphasis of Imbolc is on light. It is a simple yet powerful ceremony marked with white candles standing in a bowl of water, symbolizing the emergence of light from the feminine waters.

The weather of the season may dictate that the ceremony is performed indoors. As it is strongly identified with the hearth, this would be entirely appropriate. It certainly makes lighting and handling the candles much easier. However, there is nothing to stop you attempting the whole thing outside.

You need to be aware that any form of healing ritual - even one as gentle as this - can become quite powerful. This is not something to worry about, but it is worth keeping in mind so that you are not taken by surprise. You should always ask permission of a specific person if you wish to offer them healing. Healing for groups, whole countries, or the Land works on a different level.

For the ceremony, you will need:

- A bowl of water.
- A glass of spring water.
- White candles (these should be mounted in the bowl prior to starting the ceremony). Use either three to represent the triple nature of the goddess or nineteen to represent the number of those who tended her sacred flame.
- White flowers such as snowdrops. As you should never pick flowers from the wild, grow some in a pot - you will know it is time for the ceremony when the flowers open.
- Incense (jasmine is a suitable fragrance).
- A lighter or matches.
- A poem or chant in honour of Brigid.

After the ceremony, ground yourself with a light meal. White bread and cheese made from the milk of a sheep or goat followed by yoghurt, cakes with white icing, or white chocolate are ideal. If you need a drink, finish off the spring water and be sure to offer a portion to the Goddess.

The Ritual

Perform the appropriate opening. When this is done, walk deiseal from the east to the north-east, the place of Imbolc. Face the centre of your circle.

I come to this place at the time when all around is cold and slow, waiting for the hidden fire of spring - the secret in the womb of the Goddess that will melt the snow and ice with the first stirrings of new life.

Forests and hills awaken to her call. Creatures hear her whispers. All wait in anticipation as the moon waxes and the darkness recedes once more.

The pure white snowdrop of Imbolc, shining bright, sweeps away the dark days of winter, as I grow stronger with the coming light. I, too, hear the call.

The threefold Goddess,
Maiden, Mother, and Crone -
I welcome her as Brigid,
Goddess of Fire and Water,
Daughter of the Dagda,
Child of the Tuatha Dé Danaan.

Brigid,
Sacred Goddess of the snake,
Sacred Goddess of the rowan,
Sacred Goddess of the Grove,
I answer to your call.

Blessed Lady of Fire,
Of healing and spoken word,
I light these candles in your honour.

Step into the centre of the circle and light the candles in the bowl of water.

As you melt the winter with your breath,
You sweep away the dark days and all that is outworn.

Lift the glass of spring water.

Blessed Lady of Water,
Mother of wells and streams,
I drink this water in your honour
As you wash away all that is old
And restore the natural flow of my life once more.

Drink. Pause awhile, and then step back.

I will soon feel the returning Sun, as the light becomes stronger each day.

As this happens so will my inner light burn brightly, renewed again as the Goddess changes the Land to green once more.

Brigid, guardian of the flame, of Bards, and of healing, I ask that you send your healing energies to [*name of person(s), animal(s), place(s) to which you wish to send healing*].

Place the snowdrops by the bowl.

Sit in meditation. Feel the healing powers flow from your circle out into the world, feel them spiralling ever outwards touching all. Feel how the elements of Brigid's fire and water work within you and all about you.

When you are ready, come out of meditation and stand once more in the north-east of you circle.

I walk this circle three times to honour the mighty Lady of Fire and Water.

Walk the circle three times. A poem or a chant you have written in her honour could be read out as you walk.

As I close my circle this day, I thank Brigid for her healing and protection of our world.

When you are ready, close your circle in the appropriate way.

SPRING EQUINOX

The spring equinox is a fleeting moment of balance. Night and day, light and dark, inner and outer - all these things and so much more stand, at that brief moment, in equality. As this is a solar ceremony, this balance is symbolized by the moment when the waning powers of winter are evenly matched by the waxing powers of summer.

Balance is important to us all in so many ways. This ceremony celebrates that, yet also makes it clear that balance is not static, but achieved by accepting and living with the cyclical nature of existence. If balance were static, nothing would progress and nothing new could be learned. It is in the conclusion of each cycle and venturing on the next, that we find a completeness is achieved.

At each equinox, we pause for an instant in the act of crossing a threshold. We stand poised in acknowledgement of the moment before stepping from one realm to another. In crossing the threshold at the spring equinox, which we must if we are to be a part of the cycle, we leave behind the enclosed and contemplative world of the Winter King, which for us is centred upon the hearth. From there, we move towards the open and active realm of the Summer King that is centred upon the forest grove.

We pause on the threshold because we need that moment to reflect on the fact that our sojourn in one realm is, amongst other things, a preparation for our work in the next. The hearth work, the closeness of relationships, and the inner journeys we have made during the six months just passed will have taught us much that we can use to guide us as we step forth into a more physically active part of our lives. The parallel with the larger cycle of journeys between the Outworld and the Otherworld is clear to see.

Along with this acknowledgement of the importance of what we bring with us from the confines of the hearth and from our journeys to the inner worlds is an awareness of the great potency of the youth of the year. Those heady breaths of fresh, clean, spring air we take as we stand in the doorway are intoxicating harbingers of the Mabon - the solar hero, Arthur, with all the wild and budding world before him.

There is a great and rising power here. The whole world feels it and celebrates. Each year, at this time, there will be a day when you know from the sunshine and the bird song, from the feel of the air, from the very vibrancy of the Land, that winter is at an end and a new power is coming. This may well be earlier than the equinox, but it is formally celebrated at this time. Yet this power is nothing without the blessing of Sovereignty, the Goddess of the Land. To her, both Kings owe allegiance. And although they contend one with the other to be her champion, their reigns are complementary - providing a balanced whole throughout the course of each year.

Sovereignty is also mistress of swords and Caladvwlch is the symbol of her authority in this world. Known more commonly as Excalibur, it is a sword that bestows great power on whosoever it is gifted. In granting it to Arthur, the Goddess did much to heal the Land at a time of great dis-ease and division for in Arthur we find both summer and winter personified. This it was that gave him great strength; this that brought peace, stability, and balance; this that finally overwhelmed him. Yet even in all the chaos that surrounded the end of his reign, Arthur remained undefeated for he had achieved what needed to be done at that time.

If the waters of your mind are still enough, you will see the sword reflected there, offered to you as a gift. Through it, you may draw the power of the Land. However, remember that with such power comes great responsibility - a responsibility for the fertility of both the Land and the spirit. The sword may only be used in the service of others and never yourself. Abuse its power and it loses its potency. Abuse its power and you harm only yourself.

Preparation

Working in service of the Land is a central tenet of druidic practice. It is no easy task, but its rewards are enormous. One way in which this can be celebrated is by using the fruits of the earth. This works on many levels. Wine, for example, is the stored and matured wisdom of seasons passed and can readily be used to drink a toast to the coming King. Alternatively, if you prefer not to drink alcohol, fruit juice is equally potent and acceptable.

Seed, the stored potential of the past and symbol of the young solar hero's potency, can be sown. This can be interpreted literally, sowing the seeds of native wildflowers for example. More widely, it can be taken to mean something like putting out seed for the birds. On the other hand, perhaps you would want to plant the seeds of an idea in others, inspiring them to serve the Land.

Whatever you choose, make this sowing of the seed, this use of past wisdom a symbolic and literal part of your ritual and of your life at this time. After all, without the planting of a seed there can be no harvest. And without a harvest, there can be no seed.

For the ceremony, you will need:

- Spring flowers, in a pot if there are none growing wild where you make your circle.
- Water.
- Something to represent Air, for example a feather.
- A light and dark stone. It is possible to find a single stone that is composed of light and dark materials, but two stones of contrasting colour will do as well.

After the ceremony, ground yourself with a light meal. Perhaps a bit of cauliflower cheese and an apple with some wine or fruit cordial.

The Ritual

Perform the appropriate opening. When this is done, walk deiseal from the east right round your circle back to the east, the place of the spring equinox. Face the centre of your circle.

I have reached a time of equality, a time of balance, at the moment before the darkness gives way to the light.

The days will grow longer and the nights grow shorter until balance is attained once more at the autumn equinox.

As I feel the energies of spring, I give thanks once more to the Goddess for the gift of life and light. With this gift comes awakening and the promise of summer. Before all this comes fertile growth and strength within the Land and myself.

The Summer Lord shows once more that he is restored. I give thanks to the Sun King as my life is renewed each year. New seeds are planted, inspiration awakened in me, and the germination of life energies spiral around me once more.

Walk the circle three times and as you do, chant:

Power of the Sun,
Power of the Moon,
Power of the day,
Power of the night,
Power of the dark,
Power of the light.

Repeat three times, once for each circuit you make.

Stand in the centre of your circle.

I honour:

Ygerne the Goddess and Modron;

Myrddin the divine vision seeker, true guardian of the Land, who teaches us how to journey in the Forest and seek our own wisdom;

The Lady of the Lake, guardian of the inner realms of mystery, and giver of the sword, Caladvwlch.

Meditate on the mystery that is the sword for a while.

The silent wolf withdraws,
The crane flies lazy circles,
The hare, thrice blessed, dances in the dew.

It is the time of the Goddess as she walks the Land. Flowers bloom at each step she takes. Buds open and a carpet of green is everywhere seen. All of the Land is fertile once more.

The seeds of light planted at Imbolc now show signs of life, as day and night are balanced once more. Soon the light will spin brighter, and whispers of the spring breezes will transform the rhythm of the season. Winter's cloak is cast aside.

Soon I will hear the song of faerie on the air. Winds will blow warm once again and I will feel the magic of creation.

When you are ready, close your circle in the appropriate way.

BELTANE

The original meaning of the name of this ceremony is lost to us, although it is most probably the 'fires of Bel'. Bel is a Celtic god found throughout the whole of the ancient Celtic world under various names such as Belenos, Beli, and Bíle. He was highly regarded, a solar deity who was 'Father of Gods and Men' and consort of the Mother Goddess.

The major feature of Beltane, like Imbolc, is fire. In this case, however, it is heat rather than light that is important. It was a time for the renewal of the perpetual hearth fires that were to be found in every home. These would be extinguished, the hearths cleared, cauldrons scoured, fire dogs cleaned, the house generally tidied, and all set new and fresh. The fire would then be relit by Druids from torches carrying flame from the ceremonial bonfire - each household thereby receiving a blessing from Sun and Druid alike.

The lighting of the ceremonial bonfires and the rekindling of the hearth fires probably marked the beginning and end of the formal parts of Beltane. However, much else went on, both formal and informal, that centred on the Bel Fires. Leaping through flames (or over the embers at the edge for the less nimble and adventurous) was one of these.

Leaping was done for many reasons, but it was essentially to bring good fortune. Fire leaping was not confined to Beltane, however, as it is well documented that folk leapt the summer solstice bonfires, there being descriptions from Ireland in the late eighteenth century.

The leaping was based in the belief that the Bel fires had magical powers and that the flames destroyed those powers hostile to humanity, purified the air, and allowed people, animals, and plants to thrive and become fertile. In some areas, it was the custom to build two fires and drive livestock between them. It must have been a frightening prospect for the animals but there is evidence to suggest that it was an effective way of killing the parasites that would have thrived on beasts confined during the winter.

Another theme of this final spring ceremony is fertility in its widest sense - the generative light and heat of the Sun symbolized by the fires. In later centuries, this became part of folk culture in the May dances that evolved from the less formal aspects of the Beltane celebrations.

May dancing, when looked at carefully, reveals a very complex pattern of movement and ritual, producing spiral patterns on the ground pierced through the centre by the pole. The circles and cycles that are set out by the dance provide conduits for the energies that lay within the earth to rise to the surface. These dances occurred in the last of the three ceremonies associated with spring, as it was essential that everything had been prepared to accept the energies raised. Fields would have been ploughed and sown, animals turned out to pasture, houses spring cleaned, and so on. This first burst of activity in the agricultural cycle would have been more or less complete. A bit like cleaning the grate and laying a new fire. Everything would then be ready and waiting for the spark of energy provided by the match.

Life has changed a great deal since the prevalence of the Beltane festivals and the May celebrations. Most people still feel the urge to get out into the open and let fresh air blow through their houses and minds, but apart from forays to the local pub to sit outside and watch Morris-dancers, there is little left of the old ceremonies that seem to have direct relevance to the present day. The World is such that the cycle of fertility has been by-passed (much to the detriment of us all) and the needs of the Earth are largely ignored.

Beltane now works on a deeper level with energies of the spirit, rather than with the earthy energies of the past. Fertility and the rising powers of spring are celebrated, honoured, and harnessed now in the context of a spiritual quest to restore something of the old ways of working with the Land. Hence, the Sidhe are welcomed from their world and the symbol of Cerridwen's cauldron of transformation is invoked.

Preparation

Preparing for this ritual should be done on two levels. At a physical or material level, you should clean your house or room. Spring cleaning seems to be outdated these days, but it is still a useful exercise. Not only does it ensure your living space is clean and fresh, it is a perfect opportunity to declutter. Go through your books, music, clothes, and other possessions. We grow out of all sorts of things and letting go of them allows us to move on more freely. It also benefits all those charity shops.

As material cleaning and clearing benefits us both physically and spiritually, so too does spiritual clearing and cleaning. Prior to Beltane is a good time to make a short retreat - just a day or a weekend is fine, allowing yourself time to declutter your head and your soul.

For the ceremony, you will need:
- May flowers.
- A crown of hawthorn.
- Two lit candles in lanterns or jam-jars to place in the north-east and the south-west of your circle.
- Garlands or hoops of greenery.
- Bright ribbons to decorate your staff.

The ceremony is followed by a feast. Keep it simple. Oatcakes are traditional fare for Beltane. To stay true to the season, the main dish could be new potatoes. They are an excellent meal on their own, topped with butter. If you need a little extra, sprinkle them with grated cheese. Rhubarb is also in season and makes an excellent crumble or an equally excellent wine.

*

A note of caution. This ritual includes an invitation to the denizens of Faerie to join your circle. These are powerful beings who live by their own rules. Please be certain that they have gone at the end of the ceremony before closing your circle. If you are uncertain about inviting them in the first place, simply pay them honour but do not ask them in.

The Ritual

Perform the appropriate opening. When this is done, walk deiseal from the east to the south-east, the place of Beltane.

I stand in the place of Fire and Air.

As the wheel turns once more to Beltane, I honour Blodeuwedd and the Horned God.

Place may flowers in the centre of the circle, in honour of the flower maiden.

Energy spirals round as once more the Horned God and the Goddess meet in sacred union. The Land dances again as they transform the world from spring into summer.

The boundaries between the worlds are thin and the realms of Faerie are close. I welcome the Sidhe once more. Hear my call across the borders of the worlds. Join my circle this day as the flowers of the hawthorn prepare for the sacred oak.

At this time of the twin fires, I radiate my light as Gwion Bach arose from Elffin's weir. Transformed once more from Cerridwen's dark cauldron into the light, I jump the fires of Beltane.

Walk round the circle from the south-east to the north-west and jump or walk between the twin flames back to the south-east.

I have walked through the gateway into summer. The Goddess has swept away all that was dark and cold in my life and filled it with warmth and light. From this moment on, the days will shimmer in sunlight. All around will grow, as the Earth becomes a blanket of green. Magical energies will fly on the breeze and whisper over the hills. The Lord and Lady are handfast once more - a divine union at the full Moon.

Sit in meditation. In your Inner Grove, see the Sidhe once more at the borders of the world; be aware of the fertility that is all around, above, and below; breathe life into your world.

When you have finished your meditation, stand and either walk or dance a spiral into the centre and back out again (being careful of the candles as you go). Feel the earth under your bare feet. Give thanks to the Earth Goddess and the Horned God for the abundance that is summer.

When you feel ready, walk round the circle to the south-east (if you did not manage to return there at the end of your outward spiral) and face the centre.

As my ritual this day is brought to a close, I honour Blodeuwedd as I did in the beginning - she who was created by magic from oak, broom, and meadowsweet; she who will transform into an owl when the borders are close once more.

When you are ready, close your circle in the appropriate way. Take particular care to thank the faerie folk and ask them to depart along with everyone else. Make sure they have gone before you finally close.

SUMMER SOLSTICE

The summer solstice ceremony is the one most associated with the Druid Way by the population at large. This is because some Druid Orders consider it the most important ceremony of the year and one that should be held in the open. However, for many Druids, this is one of the four inner ceremonies in which they celebrate their link with their path away from the public gaze. Furthermore, it is not universally regarded as the most important ceremony. Many Druids who follow a lone path (including the authors) consider the winter solstice to be a much more powerful and important ceremony.

Although the solstice is an astronomical event that takes place at a particular instant in time, the celebration of summer solstice is generally held on the longest day of the year. This is the time when the Sun, born anew at the winter solstice, reaches the very peak of its strength. The symbolic struggle between the Light and the Dark, the powers of growth and decay, the Kings of Winter and Summer, reaches this point of greatest brightness and vigour in the annual cycle.

The Mabon, child of the Goddess, has now reached his full powers. The realm of Arthur is finally at peace. We celebrate that potency and that potential because, in combination with the Goddess, it has given us all life and will ripen us all to maturity. And in that lies one of the deep truths of the Druid Way: that nothing is constant except, perhaps, the constancy with which the cycles turn. For just as the Sun reaches its greatest strength we know and accept that its powers will now fade until the Winter King gains the upper hand and reaches his full strength at the time of the winter solstice. And just as Arthur's realm knows peace, its powers are scattered in the quest for the Grail.

In this ever-turning cycle, the balance of the universe is maintained and this, too, we celebrate. For we can have no true appreciation of the Light without the Dark, we can have no proper understanding of the sanctity of Life without knowing that there is also Death. However, we should take care not to think of any of these as opposites or of supporting the dualistic systems so beloved of materialistic and empirical philosophers. These linear thinkers seem only to see things as one thing or the other. However, as the turning of the year teaches us, these things that we name for our convenience are not separable one from another.

Summer does not stand alone without reference to what comes before or afterwards. It grows out of spring and it becomes autumn, both of which help define its shape, both of which give it its unique form from year to year.

Many may find it strange to see Medraut (Mordred) included within the ritual. However, we must be careful not to use later Christian interpretations of the Matter of Britain as our route to understanding. Indeed, they have been instrumental in retarding the advances of spirit toward which Arthur strove.

From a purely historical point of view, the only references to the final battle of Arthur mention that he fought 'with' Medraut. This is highly ambiguous as it can mean 'alongside' as easily as it can mean 'against'. Moreover, if Arthur and Medraut *were* mortal enemies, what they represent, as we have already noted, should not be seen as separable opposites. They are inextricably entwined aspects of an inevitable turn of a very large cycle. Just as Arthur embodied both summer and winter, his reign was one of transformation in which opposing forces, rather than competing for the right to represent Sovereignty, were subsumed within it.

The lesson for us is plain to see. We cannot rely on others to run our lives. We cannot rely on others to be guardians of the Land. We must take up these entwined responsibilities for ourselves. Sovereignty is to be bestowed on each of us if we prove ourselves worthy, and we must stand in the full spiritual glare of the midsummer Sun and know our own hearts, embrace all the aspects of our self, and integrate them so that we may use them in service of the Land, in service of the Goddess, in service of the God.

Preparation

Many Druids perform their solstice ceremony as the Sun rises, others wait until midday. There are even some who keep vigil from the previous sunset, greeting the sun as it rises, and completing the ceremony at noon. How you approach it is up to you.

However, there are practical considerations involved with lengthy rituals. You will need to break circle to attend to bodily functions (see page 19). If you are outside, make sure you have the wherewithal to perform your ablutions to your own satisfaction and without polluting the environment. Make sure you have plenty of food and water with you, some form of sunshade, and warm and waterproof clothing. Our material bodies are important and we should care for them as much as we care for our spirit.

A further note of caution is necessary for those who wish to stay in circle for a prolonged period. You will be performing a ceremony of potent natural magic. It may satisfy the ego to be able to say you have stayed the course, but it is not something to attempt unless you have had plenty of rest beforehand as well as the opportunity to rest for several days afterwards. Nor should you attempt this if your health is less than perfect. There is no less sanctity in a day spent quietly in retreat, punctuated by the ritual observances that follow which can be used either at dawn or at midday – supplemented by others of your own that you feel are necessary.

For this ceremony, you will need:
- Summer flowers.
- A chalice.
- Water.
- Incense and burner.
- A lighter or matches.
- Oak and holly.

After the ceremony, ground yourself with a meal that honours the Sun and the summer. A salad followed by bread and honey all taken with a glass of mead or spring water is ideal.

The Ritual

Perform the appropriate opening. When this is done, walk deiseal from the east to the south of your circle, the place of the summer solstice. Turn and face the centre.

This is the time of the greatest light,
The time of Sun and flowers
When all is growing and full of song,
When I have turned outwards
To consider the path since trod and the path yet untrodden.

This is the high point of summer.

All around is full with life,
Suspended in the moment,
Waiting for that turning point of light
When all of life will change once more.

This is the season of the bee and the white hart, sacred to all Druids.

On this the lightest and shortest of all nights, the Great Mother Goddess sees the decline of the Sun once again. Each day will now get shorter. Each night will get darker and longer, until the winter solstice when I will wait once more for the birth of the Mabon, the Sun King.

The seed of light from that time has grown to fullness. Soon will come the time of harvest.

At this season of long sunny days, my outer world and waking life are complete once more, so bringing new joy to my journey.

Step into the centre of the circle to honour the deities.

Gwenhwyfar, who is the otherworldly Flower Bride and Goddess of the land;

Bedwyr, who can show us devotion and compassion through our emotions if we seek them;

Medraut, who can show us how to calm our inner turmoils and battles;

I honour you all at this time.

Step back to the south.

Today the Holly King defeats the Oak King and the year once again turns. As we reach the climax of light and the turning of the tide, the energy of the Sun sows the very seeds of the dark time to come.

Our ancestors lit bonfires at this time of mid-summer to radiate light into the coming darkness. In darkness and in light there are the seeds of each other.

Sit and meditate on this for a while. When you are ready, stand up. Walk from the south to the west and there turn outwards.

I salute the place of the Grail hallow.

Walk to the north and there turn outwards.

I salute the place of the Stone hallow.

Walk to the east and there turn outwards.

I salute the place of the Sword hallow.

Walk to the south and there turn outwards.

I salute the place of the Spear hallow.

Turn inwards with outstretched arms.

I honour the four great treasures of this land, brought to us by the Tuatha Dé Danaan long ago, from their four great cities.

As the Sun starts its descent into the west, I feel the wheel of my life has turned once more.

Memories of the Sun's light and life ignite the dark to come. The Goddess reigns supreme once more.

When you are ready, close your circle in the appropriate way.

LUGHNASAD

Lughnasad means 'the remembrance of Lugh'. The name is ambiguous and easily misunderstood. It does not commemorate Lugh, as one might think, but was started by him in remembrance of his foster mother, Tailtiu. It became a great festival lasting many weeks featuring games that included athletics events as well as displays of skill and artisanship. The last games were held in August of 1169 under the jurisdiction of Ruraidh Ó Conchobhar, the last High King of Ireland.

Tailtiu was a daughter of the Fir Bolg king of the Great Plain. She became foster mother to Lugh, a common practice in Celtic society. That Lugh should establish a great festival in honour of Tailtiu says much about his affection for her. That it should be kept to this day betokens the importance of what she did - clearing the forest of Breg single-handed for use as agricultural land, dying as a result of her labours. The Great Goddess has allowed an aspect of herself to be sacrificed in order that her new children could settle and feed themselves with skills passed on to them by her foster-child Lugh.

Lugh was the child of Cian and Eithne. Renowned for the splendour of his countenance, he is a god of all arts and crafts; a master of them all and a great teacher as well. This latter role alone makes him important to Druids, as teaching is one of their prime functions. Moreover, the teaching of the skills of mundane life is of equal importance with teaching an esoteric way - for they are interdependent things, part of a unity. The soul that tends the earth without abusing Her, walks gently and in the Light.

The principal connection between Lugh and Tailtiu is, therefore, one of agriculture. During the battles between the Tuatha Dé Danaan (the people of the goddess Dana) and the Fomorians, Lugh spares the life of Bres, a captured Fomorian leader. In exchange for this, Bres teaches Lugh about ploughing, sowing, and reaping. That Tailtiu then clears a vast forest to create fields would suggest that between them they planned to bring agricultural prosperity to Ireland. However, all such ventures have a price and Tailtiu paid in full.

So it is that Lughnasad, as well as being a festival of skill and artisanship, is a time to celebrate agricultural life. It was traditionally a time when farm hands were hired for the coming year, when animals were sold, when far flung communities came together, and when temporary marriages were made (to be ended after a year and a day if the couple did not get along under the same roof). It also marked the beginning of the harvest period that ends with the autumn equinox, the period in which cereals were cut. It is for this reason that the symbol associated with the ceremony is an ear of corn or wheat.

Sickness, death, even relationships that do not last beyond the first flush of attraction were all recognized as part of our life by our ancestors. This does not mean that they simply accepted them. Health was a thing to be cherished and skilled healers and surgeons cared for the sick and weak. The fragility of relationships was recognized and there were many ways in which associations could be formed, counselled, and dissolved without stigma or hardship to either party.

It may seem strange that such a festival of life and a time of celebration should mark the death of one so beloved as Tailtiu, but it is a recognition of death in life, of the cycle that sustains us all, and of the sacrifice made by so many on our behalf. Without the harvest, without the mowing down of the grain and grass, there can be no sustenance and no renewal. All our lives are a compromise with the wilderness, for we manage the world about us as all creatures and plants do. It is only human arrogance in assuming we know best, allied with the belief that we can live separately from the rest of the world, that causes ecological devastation.

It is right, therefore, that the fertility and life of the Land and all its creatures should be celebrated and their unity recognized, even as we cut the corn and our thoughts turn to the decay and death of the year. The sun moves westward but still blazing with glory, the great firewheel, symbol of Lugh.

Preparation

Sacrifice is often associated with death and in the case of Tailtiu, her life was the price she paid for the gift she offered. It is not necessary, however, that sacrifice should involve the giving up of one's life except in extreme circumstances - and many are willing to do so in everyday acts of heroism. However, one can only give up one's own life. To offer the life of another (human or animal) is an obscenity beyond all others.

The word 'sacrifice' means 'to make sacred' and it is a recognition of the passing of things and of the cycle that will bring them back. We cannot make any sacrifice without giving up something of ourselves in the process. Nor does sacrifice have to be grand or ceremonial. It can simply involve dedicating one's self to a Way that involves putting others first, be they animals, plants, or people.

A gift at this time of year is particularly auspicious, especially if it involves you in an act of regeneration. There are many ways in which this can be done, but remember that all sacrifice involves giving up something you treasure, be it money or time.

For this ceremony, you will need:
- Summer fruits and flowers.
- A beeswax or honey coloured candle (unlit in centre).
- Bread. (A roll will suffice. The portions given to the Land and the Sky can be put out for the birds after the ritual.)
- A chalice.
- Mead, ale, or fruit juice.
- An ear or small sheaf of corn, barley, or wheat.
- A sharp knife or scissors.
- Incense.

Although the ceremony involves eating bread and drinking mead, a meal should follow. Perhaps a leek and potato soup with cheese bread, followed, if you are lucky, by the first apple of the season.

The Ritual

Perform the appropriate opening. When this is done, walk deiseal from the east to the south-west, the place of Lughnasad. Turn and face the centre of your circle.

I honour this time of the first harvest, when the Land gives of itself, enabling me to survive.

As the Corn King prepares for his sacrifice under the sickle of the Goddess, I ask to be shown the meaning of sacrifice in my life - the secrets and mystery of rebirth as the Sun grows old and loses its strength in the shortening days to come.

Step into the centre of your circle and pick up the sheaf of corn. Either cut the ears of grain from the stalks or rub them off with your hands.

The Corn King is slain so that I may live.

This is the first harvest.

The time known as Claim-time to our ancestors.

I open myself to the energies that they may fuse with mine as the Sun makes its journey into darkness.

I honour the growing darkness at this time of Lughnasad as I honoured the time of growing light at Imbolc.

I give blessings to the God and Goddess, to Lugh and Cerridwen.

Light the central candle.

From this harvest comes life out of death.

Step back to the south-west and, facing the centre of the circle, sit in meditation for a while.

Pick up the bread and walk a sunwise spiral around your circle ending in the centre. Kneel down and break the bread in three. Give some back to the Land (place it on the ground at the centre of the circle), give some to the Sky (raise it above your head and then place it on the ground). Give the remaining third to yourself and walk a sunwise spiral out to the south-west of the circle with it. Face the centre and consume the bread.

I honour the Land and the Goddess.

I honour Tailtiu.

Fill the chalice. Pick it up and walk a sunwise spiral into the centre of your circle. Kneel down and pour a little on the ground. Raise your chalice to the sky. Stand and walk a sunwise spiral out to the south-west of the circle. Face the centre and drink from the chalice.

I give thanks to the Land and the ancestors.

Now, as the time of harvest begins, the green fields and woods of the Goddess will slowly turn brown and die. Flowers will fade and fruits will be picked.

In each of these deaths there is new life, for as the Earth Mother reaches her time, she also gives us the seeds as gifts for the coming year - the seeds of life.

With this in mind, I celebrate Lughnasad and the promise of these gifts. I honour the sacrifice made by Tailtiu. I will share my energies with others, as did my ancestors, so that all may partake of this harvest.

Send out prayers or healing to others.

When you are ready, close your circle in the appropriate way.

AUTUMN EQUINOX

The autumn equinox is a mirrored image of the spring equinox. It marks the end of the dominance of the Summer King and thus the move toward Winter's rule. Once again, all is equally balanced. Summer has gone. Winter has yet to be. Yet we move inexorably from the Light to the Dark and we need to recognize that different approaches are needed to the way in which we think and conduct our lives.

We should not equate the Light with goodness and the Dark with evil. Those are largely Christian notions based on a misrepresentation of the cycles that govern our lives and the interpretation placed on them by our pagan ancestors. The Dark is as important to us as the Light, but it requires a different way of working and a different strategy for managing.

If we look to the world about us, we see that plants and animals are preparing themselves for the coming season. Most trees begin to shed their leaves - and those that do not, have leaves that are adapted to the cold and the stronger winds. Plants start to die back and retreat beneath the ground where they are protected from frosts and over grazing. Animals stock up with food either by hoarding it or by eating more to put on extra layers of fat. Some animals will later hibernate. Everything is preparing itself for a period of quiescence when little happens in the outer world. If we are sensible, if we are properly tuned to the rhythms of the world about us, then we should try to do the same.

In the past, it was second nature for our ancestors to start building up their stores of firewood and food, to make sure their dwellings were capable of withstanding the storms of winter, to see the outer world put in order before retreating within their dwellings and their selves. There, they would take up work that could be done indoors, just as they would take up work that could be done within themselves. It was a time of weaving and repairing, a time of storytelling, a time when they were forced together and had to learn to get along. It was a time to sit quietly and think, a time of patience.

Modern conveniences isolate us from the need to respond to the changing seasons. Very few of us have to chop wood and check the thatching on the roof. Nonetheless, we should respond in other ways and think carefully about the changing of the seasons and what that means to us in both material and spiritual terms.

The Dark is not yet upon us. Winter is still just a hint on the horizon. Nevertheless, that time is now beginning and once we have harvested, we must begin to make ourselves secure, ensuring that we can withstand the winter storms. As the cycles turn outside us and carry us along, they also turn within us in our bodies and in our spirits.

This is reflected in the ceremony itself, which celebrates a mature strength that will carry us forward. We cross into the realm of winter with experience in order that we might meditate on that to broaden our understanding of the world. This so that we might have wisdom to carry forward with us at the next equinox when we venture once more into the outer world.

As with spring, the symbol of the autumn equinox is the seed. However, there is a subtle difference between the seed planted and the seed harvested. That we planted seeds in order to produce seeds that we may plant them again may seem like an endless task without point, but it is only part of a much greater cycle. No seed is exactly the same as the seed from which it has grown. Each has within it the nourishment and the memory of the previous cycle, honed down to the barest essential necessary to take that forward to a new generation.

As individuals, we carry that forward in our own developing lives. However, we also carry it forward from generation to generation so that it lives on beyond us. That is why the ceremony is based round the Grail. The Grail is seed and harvest, it is wisdom incarnate, it is personal Sovereignty, and it is the means by which we heal. Now that the Land has been tended and prepared for the winter, there is time for us to seek out this most elusive of goals.

Preparation

We can see an analogy with the need to honour the cycle from seed to seed in the debate over food. Organic food is grown in sympathy with Nature - it is one of the most basic and powerful acts of magic of which we are all capable. Genetically modified foodstuffs on the other hand break the cycle of development. If that should happen – with food or in a wider sense - wisdom is lost, our strength is gone, and we will wither.

This is reflected more broadly in the way we must choose our path and work within it. Drawing bits and pieces from other paths just because they suit our fancy is damaging to the path and to those that follow. This is not to say that the path we choose cannot evolve and produce many distinct forms that cross-fertilize and preserve the vigour of the original form. It does not mean that at times one path will not be changed by another. It does not mean that we cannot look at and come to understand other paths. It does not mean that the path we chose is the 'best' path. Tomatoes are no better than fish. However, fish genes have no place in tomatoes.

In celebrating the cycle that allows us to sow and gather and sow again, we are celebrating the gift of the Goddess. It is a gift of both body and spirit that we tamper with at our peril.

For this ceremony, you will need:
- Apples.
- Berries from the hedgerows (hawthorn, blackberries).
- Water in a bowl (and a small towel).
- Red, gold, and green candles (if working indoors).
- Bread (see note for previous ritual).
- Mead, wine, or fruit juice.
- Flowers.

Follow the ceremony with something like a savoury bread and butter pudding (made with finely chopped leeks and topped with cheese). Excellent on its own, it can also be eaten with salad. Finish off with fruit such as damsons or plums.

The Ritual

Perform the appropriate opening. When this is done, walk deiseal from the east to the west, the place of the autumn equinox. Turn and face the centre of your circle.

At this place on the wheel,
Before the gates of the full grown year,
I honour this, the time of the second harvest,
Song-time, when all growth slows.

I dedicate myself to the seeking of the Grail in my life, letting its light flow into me as the dying light of the year fades into the west.

I will heal myself with sacred water from the Grail at this time, and in so doing will send out healing to the world, for the power of the Grail allows all to be healed.

Step forward, dip your hands in the bowl of water, and gently wash your face. As you do so, feel the power of the water healing your hurts and restoring your energy. Stand and raise your hands. Turn deiseal to face east, south, west, and north, sending healing to each of the four quarters in turn. Step back from the centre before walking deiseal round the circle's edge, back to your place in the west.

I honour Peredur the Grail Guardian.
He offers us wisdom and insight if we seek within our own waters of the Grail, so bringing healing to our wasteland.

I honour Angharad of the Golden Hand.
Her compassion is an example to us in our nurturing of all things within the Land, the Sea, and the Sky.

I honour Nimuë the faerie weaver.
She offers us the gift of intuition and initiation and teaches us self-renewal in our meditations, visions, and dreams.

Light the candles.

At this time of the autumn equinox, I mark the balance between light and dark, day and night.

It is from this moment that the dark waxes and the light wanes, this being the ebb and flow of the yearly cycle.

Without this cycle, there would be no rebirth of the Sun at the winter solstice.

Step into the centre of your circle and salute the west, the place of the chalice.

To the waters of the West, the place of the ancestors and the sacred salmon;

To the blessed harvest and the sacred grains;

To the Goddess Cerridwen and the cauldron of rebirth;

I share this sacred feast in their honour.

The goblet of mead is first given to the Land and the Goddess before drinking of the harvest yourself.

The bread is broken. A segment is given to the Land and the Goddess, then to yourself.

Sit in meditation for a short time. Think of what you have harvested in your life this past year, from ideas sown at the spring equinox. Consider the importance of the Way you have chosen.

Feel the axis about which everything turns, feel the moment of balance in both time and space.

When you have finished, stand up and step back to your place in the west. Walk the circle deiseal from the west to the east.

Pause a moment, before moving deiseal from the east to the west.

The great wheel has turned once more.

When you are ready, close your circle in the appropriate way.

SAMHAIN

Samhain is not about death, as many suppose; it is about the dead. There is a difference. If there is a place on the wheel of the year for death, it is the autumn equinox, but it is so much a part of the process of living, so much a part of the ongoing cycle, that it is accorded no special status. The dead, however, do have their own festival for they are the ancestors, our loved ones, and it is only right that we pay our respects and set aside a special time to honour them.

This coincides with what ancestral Celts considered to be the end of summer (which is the meaning of the word 'Samhain') and the end of the agricultural year. It is indicative of their attitude to death that the end of the cycle is not death itself (the harvest) but the state of being dead (fields cleared and ready for the next year).

With the summer gone and the final preparations for winter made, more time would be spent indoors. Inevitably, people would reflect on the year just gone. Settling into their places about the hearth where they would spend a great deal of their time over the coming months, they would be conscious of those spaces where once sat the family members and friends who had died since last Samhain. With all the work of the year done and everything ready for the coming cycle, there would be time then to tidy up their past lives, time to settle differences, time to pay debts, and time to remember.

Today, most people have a strange attitude towards the dead. We can none of us doubt that it is painful in the extreme to lose a loved one, even when we are prepared for it. It is therefore right and proper that we mourn. However, what we mourn is our loss and our pain and, some might say, our misfortune at being left behind.

This is not to say that we should crave death. It is simply a recognition of the fact that when the time comes we should embrace it as readily as we embrace the rest of life. It is part of the natural order of our lives, part of the cycle of our being, and like any part of the cycle, it marks a transition from one phase of being to another. Many present day observances at this time of year are faint echoes of that.

Hallowe'en is perhaps the most obvious and strongly connected festival. Unfortunately, it has been much corrupted in recent decades, especially by the Americanized version with its emphasis on horror and extortion. However, if we look at how Hallowe'en has been observed in the past we find many customs that show signs of very ancient practice.

Originally, it was a time for Guising (going masked) and part of the cycle of pagan mystery plays and dances. Originally, men would disguise themselves as women, women as men, young as old, old as young, living as dead, and dead as living. This custom has its roots in a belief that the dead return to commune with the living at a time when the normal boundaries between this world and the Otherworld are dissolved.

There is nothing sinister in this - no ghosts, monsters, or rotting corpses. It was simply a time to make a final reckoning of what had been lost, to honour and give thanks for the time that had been shared, to settle debts (from which trick or treat has evolved), and to make a final goodbye so that both the living and the dead could move on in their respective worlds.

This applies equally to relationships and associations, be it the end of a marriage or leaving school. The first Samhain following the event is the time to take stock - celebrate what was good, reflect on what was bad, and learn from both.

For all these reasons, the ceremony at Samhain is the most solemn of the eight seasonal rituals - our remembrance of those departed cannot help but be emotionally difficult for us. However, it is also a celebration of all that they have given us in the past and all that they can still do to help us on our chosen path.

Preparation

Although a sprig of yew is appropriate for the ceremony, it is not always easy to obtain. Despite its longevity, the native yew is now rare. If you have no yew of your own, find a tree near you and befriend it. It may even offer a sprig at the appropriate time. If not, carry its spirit and blessing with you at Samhain. These connections are known in the realm of spirit and they serve us well.

If you handle Yew, make sure you wash your hands before preparing food or eating. The toxicity of Yew is still little understood and some individuals are more susceptible than are others. Casual contact is not known to cause ill effects, but it is better to be safe than sorry when it comes to ingestion.

Given the nature of the ceremony, many Druids prefer to work indoors. The weather can be bad and the energies raised can be difficult. Far better to be in a space where you are comfortable and in control. You should also be aware of the fact that if you do your ceremony indoors on Hallowe'en, you are going to be disturbed by 'trick-or-treaters' knocking on your door. Work late or choose another day.

For this ceremony, you will need:
- A sprig or wand of yew.
- A cauldron.
- Vervain or other herbs.
- Incense (juniper or clove being most appropriate).
- Bread (see note for Lughnasad).
- Mead or fruit juice in a chalice.
- A candle for the centre (black or some other dark colour).
- Photos or mementos of departed loved ones.
- A tarot deck, runes, scrying bowl, or your favoured divining tools.

You will need good, solid fare afterwards to ground yourself. Cheese, potato, and onion pie with fresh baked bread followed by apples or pears (perhaps baked together in a crumble with lashings of custard) will replenish and warm you.

The Ritual

Perform the appropriate opening. When this is done, walk deiseal from the east to the north-west, the place of Samhain. Turn and face the centre of your circle.

This is the time of seed-fall when the borders of the worlds are close, the veiled doorway to the Summerland but a single step away.

As I approach the gateway towards winter, season of darkest-depths and the dead, I prepare myself to meet the Dark Goddess, the Cailleach.

As Crone, she moves across the Land, stripping it to its bare bones, harrowing the ground in readiness for what will come. For before birth must come death, before light must come the darkness, before movement must come the stillness.

I stand here this Samhain night on the borderland. I wait to meet Gwyn ap Nudd, Lord of Annwfn, as the old year spirals ever-inwards towards renewal.

And at the year's very end the Cailleach will unlock the doors between the worlds from this side, Gwyn ap Nudd from the other.

Close your eyes to this world and visualize the strand between the worlds.

As the gates to the Otherworld stand open this night, I ask the ancestors to join me, to guide, and to gift me inner vision as the year moves towards rebirth.

Turn outwards and with arms outstretched call to the ancestors.

Come enter dear ones to this sacred space.

Turn inwards and step into the centre of your circle.

Light the central candle as a guide.

Sit, facing outwards towards the north-west.

Wait for the ancestors.

When you feel the time is right, place the yew next to the candle and step out to the north-west. Turn and face inwards.

The yew symbolizes regeneration. As I honour it, I honour the beloved dead, for in this is an initiation of life and death and life.

Step back into the centre.

Break the bread. Give some to Land and some to the ancestors.

Make a libation of mead or fruit juice to the Earth, and then to the ancestors.

Now partake of both for yourself.

As the world now slips into a place of no-time, we reach a moment of gathering. Shadowy spirit animals roam the land. The world of the Sidhe is also just a glimpse away.

As the Rowan protects us as we journey through into our future, so the Yew helps us to communicate with our loved ones.

Now is the time for divination and for lighting the fire of hope in my own wasteland - a time of release and renewal, letting the truth surface in the flame.

Sit in meditation. Give blessings and prayers to all those departed ones you wish to remember at this time.

This meditation might also include giving away energies in your life that you no longer need or desire. Consign them to you inner cauldron where they will be dissolved.

When you have finished, stand and return to the north-west of the circle.

Before closing, you might like to perform some divination work for the coming year. Sprinkle some vervain to help you see more clearly with your psychic eyes or sit in meditation with your ancestors on the threshold of your journey to the centre of the maze, feeling the passing of one season into the next as the year crosses the threshold into winter.

When you are ready to finish this ritual you must make sure you thank all those seen and unseen, remembering to ask them to leave. If you do not feel they have left, repeat your plea until all feels clear.

I thank all the ancestors, those seen and unseen who walked with the living this night. Depart this circle now in peace. Be at rest. Farewell.

When you are ready, close your circle in the appropriate way.

WINTER SOLSTICE

The time of the winter solstice has been marked and celebrated by many peoples for thousands of years. It was traditionally an open-air ceremony on sites with orientations towards the solstice sunrise and, in some cases, the sunset as well. Newgrange in County Meath, Ireland (built some 4,500 years ago) was carefully constructed so that the light of the rising midwinter Sun passes along the upper gallery of the approach passageway, straight into the central chamber. At Stonehenge, the rising sun on midwinter's day can be seen through the south-east trilithon.

Druids, of course, did not build these monuments, although they doubtless knew of their existence and function. However, they do establish the antiquity and importance of the event. And we know the winter solstice was still supremely important through into the historical era as the Christian Church appropriated it at the end of the third century AD as the moment of the nativity of the Christ.

For many Druids, the authors included, the ceremony at winter solstice is by far the most important of the annual celebrations. It is the turning point of the whole year where one inner cycle ends and the next begins. The ritual is imbued with mystery and wonder, celebrating birth and rebirth, healing, sovereignty, and a commitment to the Land. It is also the ideal time to make and to reaffirm one's vows as a Druid.

Although many consider this the most important ceremony of the year, it is also the most difficult on which to expound. This is because it is the most personal. Whereas the other annual ceremonies treat equally with our relationship between the material and spiritual, the winter solstice ceremony is almost entirely inward. It revolves around our personal mystery, our relationship with ourselves - the place where each of us must stand alone in the dark.

There is nothing maleficent in this; it is simply something we must all learn to face. At its most exoteric, it is about coping with the problems that life throws at us, especially those for which we have a genuine responsibility. Esoterically, it is the moment when we reach the centre of the spiral and there have to come to terms with our true selves, perhaps the hardest task of all on any spiritual journey.

That darkness is to be found at the heart of all mysteries and there, if we are ready, we will find two things. The first is that no matter who or what we are, there are certain things in both our material and spiritual lives that can only be done by us and for which we alone have responsibility. The second is that in the very heart of darkness there is light. It is the light of birth, rebirth, and a commitment to the Druid Way.

During the ceremony, the cycle of death and rebirth is observed, the apparent death of the Sun is mourned, the lights extinguished, the greatest dark of the year embraced. It is in this deepest darkness that we are alone. However, the moment is not endless, for the fire is lit and the Sun returns. It is not yet strong, but its light is the hope and promise of a new year and a new reign.

All this is embodied in the ceremony in the person of the Mabon, the sacred child born to Modron, the Great Mother Goddess. As his birth is always on the shortest day (and feasted after he has survived for three days), he is clearly a solar deity. Much of the myth cycle of the Mabon has been lost to us in direct form, but we can glimpse much of it from the early Arthurian tales.

Arthur too is a solar deity who comes into his own on the shortest day, drawing the sword from the stone and thereby demonstrating his unique power over the two great symbols of summer and winter, the symbols of the Land and of Sovereignty.

With him in his quest to unite and heal the Land he is aided by Gawain in his guise as a green man who achieves his own quest for Sovereignty in Arthur's name, bringing renewed fertility. Morgan, too, is present, watching over Arthur, protecting him from harm, bestowing further symbols upon him of her power. And, when he has broken his mortal self in her name, protecting the Land, she bears him away to be healed in Avalon.

Preparation

As this ceremony is the big one of the year, it is well worth preparing for and taking your time over. This will allow you the chance to feel the changes that are taking place, away from the commercial hustle and bustle associated with the midwinter.

Begin by decorating your house and the room where you will have your ceremony with greenery and candles (and as ever you must be careful - the last thing you want to do on the solstice is burn your house down). Do not rush this and keep it simple. Enjoy it, as it is part of a celebration of rebirth, but make sure you are conscious of why you are bringing greenery into the house.

On the day of the solstice, try to keep the whole day clear if you can. You may wish to hold a vigil outside at sunrise, touch the Land, feel the world as it comes to this moment of repose. If you can find a site where mistletoe grows, then this should be used. Unfortunately, it is all too rare in the wild. After this, rest. Spend the day meditating, relaxing, bathing, listening to gentle music, and preparing yourself for the ceremony itself. If you can, try to hold your ceremony so that the actual moment of solstice is encompassed by the darkness between extinguishing and relighting the candles.

For this ceremony, you will need:
- A lighted candle in the centre.
- A lighted candle in each quarter.
- Mistletoe.
- Incense (frankincense or sandalwood are ideal).
- A lighter or matches.

Ground yourself after the ceremony with something solid and warming like a baked potato with cheese and onion. Follow this with a mince pie or three and glass or two of mulled wine.

The Ritual

Perform the appropriate opening. When you have done this, walk deiseal from the east to the north of your circle, the place of the winter solstice. Turn and face the centre.

This is the time of the greatest dark, the time of snow and ice, when all is still and silent, when I have turned inwards to consider the path since trodden and the path yet untrodden. For this is the heart of winter.

All seems devoid of life, suspended in the moment, waiting for that turning point of light when all life will change – the moment of rebirth.

On this the darkest and longest of all nights, the Great Mother Goddess gives birth to the Sun once again.

As I wait for the birth of the Mabon, I reflect that I too have come through the darkness of the womb. I shall not fear this time, for in this darkness grows a seed of light.

At this time of starry midnight deep, my inner world and dream life are complete once more, so bringing new depth to my journey.

Pause and meditate on this.

At this time of winter solstice, I honour Arthur, the Sun King, who returns and unites us once again with the Land;

I honour Morgan, the Raven Queen, ruler of Avalon, who by her magic takes us across the waters of the lake to be healed;

I honour Gwalchmai the Green, who battled bravely with the Holly King to bring back the light and the reign of the Oak King.

Walk your circle three times to connect with these deities. Feel their energies working within you.

This is the season of the wren, king of birds, sacred to the Oak King and all Druids.

This is the season of the Oak Mistle, whose sacred berry is heal-all, seed of life on golden bough at work in the world to weave order from chaos.

This is the season of the Winter King and the divine child who will heal the Wasteland.

Tonight the year turns once again.

Step into the centre, pick up the mistletoe, and return to the north. Carry it around your circle. Extinguish the candles at the quarters as you go, starting with the north.

Step into the centre and extinguish the candle there.

Sit for a while in meditation. Feel the planet, the whole universe, as it turns about you, moving from one cycle to the next. Be aware of yourself and all that is at the heart of your being. Take as long as you like before continuing with the ceremony.

I came from the darkness of the womb, where I was created, nourished, and prepared for my birth into the light. I still carry that fertile darkness deep within me. I shall not fear the darkness, for it is but a shadow cast by my doubts standing between me and the light eternal.

Re-light the central candle.

A small light burns in the darkness.

Goddess, bless this flame that its light may herald the rebirth of the Sun.

Goddess, bless this flame that its light may herald the rebirth of the Son.

Walk the circle deiseal re-lighting the other candles, starting with the north. Return to the north.

I shall work with the Goddess and dream my future into being, for my world is ever dreamt awake, year on year.

At this time of my rebirth, I renew my covenant with the Land.

I will follow the Way in likeness of the hawk, watching keen-eyed and absorbing all into my stillness.

I will follow the Way in likeness of a tree, fixing into my being all that I have absorbed.

I will follow the Way in likeness of the Sun, sending forth warmth and light.

Pause.

By Birch, I will work to:
know and preserve the history of our way and our people;
know and protect the places of our way;
express the Druid Way through all the actions of my life;
seek out and preserve the ancient wisdom;
learn and understand the sacred word;
open doors with the power of the word;
be a force for good in the world.

Pause.

By Yew, I will work to:
know, understand, and respect the trees and their ways;
know, understand, and respect all creatures and their ways;
know compassion and, in accordance with my own skills, heal the
    hurts of the world;
converse with our ancestors;
explore and come to know the Summerlands;
understand the mysteries of death and rebirth;
cultivate intuition;
open the doors of time and there travel freely;
know ways of understanding what is to be.

Pause.

By Oak, I will work to:
investigate and understand the universe;
offer good counsel and advice;
develop my intellect;
seek balance in my life;
seek wisdom in my life;
teach;
be truth;
generate and regenerate.

Pause.

In all this I ask for Arianrhod's blessing and guidance - She, who is the Goddess of the Silver Wheel, of birth, initiation, and reincarnation; She, who weaves her silver thread through my life leading me to Caer Arianrhod the place of rebirth, where I will experience true illumination.

Light in darkness. The star of insight.

When you are ready, close your circle in the appropriate way.

PART TWO

THE LAND

RITES OF PASSAGE

The ceremonies of the eightfold year, which are governed by the Sun and Moon, are to be found reflected in the ceremonies that are governed by the Earth. This is true on both literal and metaphorical levels. The varying positions of the Sun and Moon provide, as we have seen in the previous section, the timetable for the Sky cycle. However, this relationship with the Sky is also indicative of the scope and tenor of those ceremonies. They mark the pattern of our relationship with the wider community of life, the universe itself, and the universal aspect of spirit.

The rites of passage in this section of the book are those that are governed by the Earth. They follow the same cycle of birth, growth, maturity, death, and rebirth that is to be found in the ceremonies of the eightfold year, but the emphasis is different and the focus is much narrower. What is more, the turning of the Earth does not dictate the times at which these ceremonies occur. Rather, they are linked to our selves and mark the pivotal occasions of our lives.

There is a connection, however, albeit far less overt than those that guide us to the inner mysteries. The rites of passage connect with the Earth in that just as our relationship with the Earth is personal, so they celebrate our personal journey and the relationships we make and break with others and the Earth along the way. The focus here is on the material aspect of our being, not only recognizing that our being has a material dimension as well as a spiritual one, but also reminding us that we live very firmly in that material dimension.

The validity of the rituals that follow as ancient rites is wholly open to question. We simply do not know how our Celtic ancestors made formal celebration of the major events of their lives. We do not even know for certain which events they considered important, although we can make an educated guess. For example, people who live by a lunar calendar, as did our ancestors, do not calculate or celebrate their birthdays in the same way as people who live by a solar calendar. They tend to have a collective 'birthday' at the same time that they celebrate their new year - which is why we have not included birthdays as a rite of passage.

It is also the case that our perspectives are different. Our ancestors may well have celebrated the onset of female menses, even if it was as a women only rite, but present day society's attitudes to sexual being are hugely distorted and we felt it better to omit this. This is not to say it is not important to the individual involved, but we feel it to be a private matter.

For all that, we do know one thing for certain - our ancestors were a highly spiritual people who loved to party. Moreover, there are tantalizing glimpses in the old tales of certain rites of passage. We do not know if these were the norm or whether they were included in these tales because they were out of the ordinary. However, from a study of law texts and other sources more prosaic than the myths and legends, we have derived a list of eight important events that we believe should be marked by ceremony and, where appropriate, by celebration.

This set of rituals is by no means exhaustive any more than they are prescriptive. The personal nature of what is celebrated - that is, your own life - may prompt you to add others (as indicated above) and to change those that we offer to better suit your own circumstances. However, we have chosen what follows for a number of reasons.

To begin with, it is because they are familiar but all too often neglected. This is not to say that they are ignored - as any glance at the list that follows will show. They are neglected in the sense that they have become both devalued and disconnected. The reasons for this are complex, but in essence we have forgotten why these events are so important and our attempts to mark them have become entirely self-referential - we celebrate an event because it is that event and for no other reason. In losing the connectedness, the deeper reason why we celebrate such events, their value to us and to our community has diminished.

Our lives are not linear. All living things follow a cycle through the duration of a lifetime. Moreover, in each cycle we undergo a number of essential transitions that shape us as social beings. In human society, there are a number of these transitions that are common to us all. We are born, so making a full transition into this world from the Other; we are named and thus recognized as a person in our own right; most of us reach an age when we become capable of taking full responsibility for our actions; we assert our independence and make our own way in the world; we commit ourselves to relationships beyond those to which we were born; relationships end; we die and make our return to the Otherworld; our material remains are disposed of.

These events occur and recur in complex cycles, more so today as the structure of society is more complicated than ever it was. They also run one into another and each contains elements of the others. Dying, for example, is to bring relationships to end in this world just as it is to assert a form of independence. This is one of the ways in which these events, these rites of passage, connect. They are the experiences of a single cycle of life that help to give it unity and mark its evolution. This alone invests them with enormous value and makes them worth celebrating in a coherent fashion. However, there is so much more.

Not only do we experience these as events that unify our own lives, but they are also the experiences of others in which we can all share. Whatever culture or religion you consider; these events are held to be of great importance. They highlight the key moments not only in our personal development, but also in our social development. As such, they are marked with formal ritual, no matter how intimately.

Given that ancestral Celtic society was tribal, personal and social development were one and the same thing. It is only in comparatively recent times that these have been considered separate rather than distinct, contributing to the disconnection and devaluation we have already mentioned.

The whole question of connectedness is fundamental to the Celtic metaphysic and to being Druid. There is not room here to elaborate on that, but we can state with a great deal of confidence that not only were these rites of passage celebrated, they were also moments of communal celebration in the widest sense of the phrase. They were rituals that bound the person to the community, the community to the person, community with community, and the person to themselves.

Communion is essential. It is no use expressing a belief in the connectedness of all things if we do not actively participate. Connection cannot be passive. It has to be two-way; otherwise, one's existence first becomes selfish and then progresses toward psychosis. Connection must also be constant. We cannot turn it on and off no matter how guarded and careful we may be in order to protect ourselves. We all filter our experiences, especially now that the pain of the whole world is so easily brought into our homes on an hourly basis.

Part of the filtering process is ritual. No matter how trivial seeming or brief, each time we enact a ritual properly we create a sacred space, a protected place in which we can explore, understand, and reaffirm our connectedness. In the Sky ceremonies of the eightfold year, we commune with the larger world. In the Earth cycle, during our rites of passage (and at other times), we commune with ourselves and with our fellow travellers.

Communing with ourselves is often neglected even though we recognize the wisdom of the ancient saying, 'know thyself'. It is not an easy path to travel, but if we do not do it, we neglect a large portion of what it is to be Druid, for being Druid is just that - it is something we are, not something we do in addition to what we are. The rituals of the Earth cycle are one means by which we define the parameters of what we are. They give us pointers to the rough shape of our being.

Our communion, however, must extend beyond our self and the Way we follow. No matter how intensely we follow the Greenway, the path by the Hedge and through the Forest, we are part of a larger community of both spirit and matter. Our actions bind us to that community in all its complexity and the nature of our actions help to shape it as well as our place within it. If we are true to what we profess (and that truth is partly to be found within the sacred spaces we create) then that community will be the better for it.

Each of the rites of passage also marks the completion of a cycle within a cycle. They are transitions, initiations, the moments of rebirth (and often of revelation) that we all experience when we open ourselves to the sacred. Certain of these have, perforce, to be conducted by others on our behalf, but that neither lessens nor invalidates their importance to us - one reason why we encourage people to plan their own funerals. This highlights the absolute duty of care we have when performing these rites on behalf of others. That is also why these rites are not about binding people to anything unless they have specifically given their consent (as in marriage).

Because they are personal, relating to the self and to our immediate family and friends, the shape and texture of these rituals is different from those we have offered for the eightfold year. Nor do they need to be opened and closed in such a formal way. Such formality and ceremonial is not always convenient or, indeed, appropriate. Where a circle is considered proper, it can be visualized - cast by the mind of the presiding Druid. After all, we are not dealing with cosmic powers that require a robust portal any more than we need protection as we work.

What we are dealing with here is a simple if profound link between ourselves and the Mother Goddess, who will always offer what protection we may perhaps need. Even with the larger rituals such as marriage and burial, we are concerned with a focus on people rather than a focus on deity - a focus on family and the personal.

Furthermore, these rituals together are a circle, the circle of our lives, constructed as we live. They are an integral part of our material and spiritual existence. We are not attempting to connect with or celebrate the wider existence of the universe (although that connection exists in that we are all part of that wider existence). Rather, we are celebrating ourselves. This is in no way egotistical. It is an acknowledgment of our personal being in a way that links us with the universe, that nurtures our spirit, and that brings balance into everyday existence.

This is all too often ignored by those who seek a spiritual path. Their whole focus is on the Sky, on the mystical experience, on the glamour of the big ritual. We must certainly be aware of the larger picture, but as we have mentioned before, we cannot successfully explore that larger domain unless we have an understanding of our own being in its normal, everyday existence.

By celebrating the normal, the inevitable events of our lives, we make contact with what is important - the relationships we have with other people, with our community, with the planet. If we neglect that, if we ignore the wisdom and the truth that is to be found by the hearth, we cannot hope to find the wisdom and truth of the universe at large, let alone cope with it.

This does not mean that one set of rituals is more important than the other. Even a quick reading will show that they are different takes on a single theme. Winter solstice is a celebration of the birth and rebirth of the Sun, which is symbolic of life on a large scale. It is a powerful and important time. So too is the birth of a child. Yet that is to be celebrated on an intimate scale, in keeping with the fragility of the newly arrived soul. The intent is no less powerful or reverential, simply in scale with and appropriate for the event.

The same is true for the rest of the ceremonies. They are reflections, one of the other. Not exact, but as if seen in the faintly rippled waters of a misty lake. We see the world at large but in a form that better suits our being. The correspondences are not absolute, but the principle is there and is an indication of the way in which we are but a part of the whole.

*

We realize that the circumstances of your life may make some of the rituals that follow either irrelevant or inappropriate. They are offered only as a guide. Where necessary, you must create your own, empowering yourself and bringing your own rites of passage to the centre of your being as Druid. For all that they may be important to you as a Druid, however, the rites that follow (and any that you may create) have no legal standing. Births and deaths must be registered with the appropriate authority. For a marriage to be legally recognized, civil proceedings must be undertaken. Divorce must go through the courts.

BIRTH

The birth of a child is a time of wonder, elation, stress, and pain. It is a time when the height of spirituality goes hand in hand with the most basic of physical concerns. It is little wonder, then, that it was an occasion of mixed feelings for our Celtic ancestors. On the one hand was the joy felt by parents, relatives, and their communities at the arrival of a new spirit. Their lives had been enriched. On the other hand was the realization that new life in this world comes only at the loss of a life in the Otherworld. The celebration of birth was accompanied, therefore, by a lament.

It is important to acknowledge this as it acts to focus our attention on the child and their journey. Birth is a fleeting moment in a lengthy cycle. A soul moves from the Otherworld to this to embark on a new portion of their journey. They have done this before, as have we all. Behind them is a wealth of experience and understanding - something you can sometimes glimpse in a young baby's eyes.

Even so, whatever any of us may bring forward from previous lives soon fades as the demands of our new existence take over. We all start each cycle afresh in order to make the best we can of the circumstances in which we find ourselves and of the time we are given.

This early phase of the journey is much influenced by parents and other relatives. Their attitudes do much to shape how the child views the world, even when only a few days old. It is important, therefore, that everyone begins as they mean to go on: gently, openly, and with love.

It is customary for gifts to be given for the child at the time of birth. Whilst material objects such as toys are always welcome, it is worth giving thought to more insubstantial but perhaps more valuable gifts. The parents, for example, should give thought to what may happen to the child in the event of their own demise. In ancestral society, many children were fostered for a while in order to strengthen community links, but also to provide for the child's welfare should anything happen to the birth parents. We are not advocating formal fostering, but it may be worth asking trusted relatives or friends to act on the child's behalf, much as the executor of a will acts to distribute the estate of the deceased. In the case of these 'foster' parents, their responsibility would be to ensure the welfare of the child during such a traumatic period, deal with all those things that a child would not be able to deal with (such as funeral arrangements), and ensure that they are settled and secure in a new life.

This is a big responsibility to lay on someone and it should not be done without great thought and much planning, but it would be a great gift of love to the child - one that we all hope will never be needed.

Welcoming a child into the family need not be confined to birth. If a child is adopted or fostered, they need to be made as welcome as possible. It also provides the opportunity for the newcomer to meet their new family in a gentle way. Whilst a baby may not be conscious on a level we understand, toddlers and older children may be daunted by such an introduction. It is important that it is kept low key and informal so that they do not feel overwhelmed.

Preparation

This short and very gentle ceremony can be performed in the birthing room or when mother and baby return home from hospital. The purpose of the rite is to welcome the new spirit into the heart of your family, therefore grandparents, siblings, and other close relatives may also like to take part.

A name for the child is not used in the ritual, as there is a separate, formal naming ceremony. However, if you wish to use your child's name, simply put it in before, or in place of, 'this new spirit'.

Soft lighting or candles are better for the new baby's eyes, but on no account use any incense or, as some people do, smudge sticks. Babies do not need their auras cleansed! Moreover, their tiny noses and lungs do not need to be polluted by smoke.

The Ritual

Making sure the baby is warm and not distressed in any way; place them in the centre of the room in a carrycot or something equally safe. Grandparents and other family members should sit around the new child, forming a protective circle.

The mother (if she is able) and father enter from the west and walk deiseal to the east to honour all that is new. They then walk the circle deiseal three times. After this, they sit either side of the child and, with arms outstretched, hold hands - the baby in the middle of this inner circle. If there is only one parent, the child can be held in their arms or a close family member could sit in. The following words can be read by either a parent or grandparent.

The Otherworld's loss is our gain.
We share their sorrow as they share our joy.

We/I welcome this new spirit to our family:
You, who have chosen to come into our lives
To grow and learn
With our love and care.

We will show you the gifts of Land, Sea, and Sky.
Be welcome among us
Child of the Goddess.
Blessed Be.

One of the parents now picks up the child and walks the circle, stopping at each family member. This allows everyone the chance to greet the new born in their own way.

When this is done, all who have joined this welcoming should be asked to visualize the light of the circle radiating out into the world, sending love and blessings to all the new spirits arriving as well as to all those departing.

NAMING

One of the first responsibilities of parents is to choose a name for their expected child. This can occasion much discussion until names are finally agreed. And, sadly, for most people it ends there. The names are entered on the birth certificate in an often busy office in a most anti-climactic way without the child being present.

Many who seek a more formal naming ceremony opt for a christening. However, christening is part of a ceremony that initiates the baby into the Christian Church. This is wholly inappropriate. One needs to be a practising Christian to opt for this (although many who are not still have their babies christened). Worse, though, is the fact that a decision is being made on the child's behalf that not even parents have a right to make. We should be allowed to choose our faith when we are old enough and informed enough to make that choice.

The naming ceremony that follows does not initiate the baby into the Druid Way. It is a formal expression to the outside world that a new soul has arrived. The birth ceremony is a family affair. And whilst it is unlikely that you would wish to invite members of the wider community to the naming, you are making an open promise to care for the child as well as bestowing a form of identity that links them to your family (by means of their surname) whilst individuating them (by means of their given names).

In bestowing that identity, parents must bear in mind a number of factors. After all, a name is a powerful gift and will have a profound influence on the person who bears it. The old tales are replete with examples of this. Be thoughtful in your choice.

There are many excellent books available to help in the search for an appropriate name. Consider the origin of the name (a Native American or Hindu name may sound good, for example, but is it really appropriate for someone not born into these cultures?); its meaning (would you really want your daughter's name to mean 'night monster'); its diminutive forms; and how it accords with the meaning and sound of your surname. Consider, too, how the child will feel and how the rest of the world will react to the names you choose.

These points are extremely important. The name is for the child and not for the parents. If we like exotic or invented names then we should adopt them ourselves (and make it clear to our children that they may do the same when they are old enough), or bestow them as magical names. This is not to say that every child should be called John or Mary, but we should take a moment to imagine to what our young lives would have been like had we been called Moonmeadow Flowerfield or Wolfmaster Strongtree.

Preparation

This is a formal ceremony, presided over by a Druid or Druids. Where only one Druid is available, they must take all the parts set out below and open it as a solo ceremony. It is preferable if it takes place outside, but this should be weighed against the health and welfare of the child.

A great deal of preparation is required if you want the ceremony to run smoothly. As you may well have guests attending to witness the event, a brief rehearsal is advised so that everyone actively involved knows where to go and what to expect. In addition, the presiding Druid needs to be familiar with the child, the parents, and needs to know the chosen names in advance.

When the child is presented to the world, common sense must prevail. It is customary to hold the child aloft, but everyone concerned must feel comfortable with this. If the presiding Druid is uncertain, it may be best to allow one of the parents to do it. Alternatively, everyone may feel happier if the child is taken round the circle to each of the quarters.

A final note. If you intend to invite deities into your circle, choose with extreme care. The child is fragile. The same goes for inviting faeries. If you want to invite them, you must invite them all. Sleeping Beauty's parents did not, and look what happened as a result.

The Ritual

Gather the family and friends into a circle, facing inwards. The presiding Druid performs the appropriate opening, enclosing everyone gathered within the circle. The Druid in the west then opens a gateway to allow the parent(s) with their baby to enter. The baby is walked deiseal around the circle three times before being taken into the centre. The Druid presiding asks the parents to enter into a state of meditation, where they visualize a pure, white light enveloping them from above. As this light falls on the baby and parents, they are surrounded by love and sacredness. This should not be hurried.

Druid 1: We have come to this place to welcome a new spirit to this world. May this child of the Goddess grow in light and love, surrounded and supported at all times by family and friends. Who takes responsibility for this tiny spirit?

Parents: We do - with all our love and devotion. We speak for our child before the four quarters, those seen and unseen, the ancestors, the Goddess and the God, the Sun, the Moon, and the Stars. We will protect this child who has come into our care.

The baby is handed to the presiding Druid.

Druid 1: May the blessings of the ancient ones be on this child.

Druid 2: May the blessings of the ancient ones be on this child.

Druid 3: May the blessings of the ancient ones be on this child.

The baby is then presented to the world.

Druid 1: Before the Goddess and the God, by Land, Sea, and Sky, and by the sacred Fire, we name this child [*child's name(s)*].

This can be followed by a magical name as well if desired. The baby is lowered. The presiding Druid then faces the parents and is flanked by the other Druids.

Druid 1: Will you allow this child to live in the joy of life?

Parents: We will.

Druid 2: Will you provide a secure yet gentle home?

Parents: We will.

Druid 3: Will you respect this child and show patience?

Parents: We will.

> *The baby is handed back to the Mother. The flanking Druids step back into the circle.*

Druid: I ask that you allow [*child's name(s)*] to choose their own path when the time arrives, just as you have also trodden the many ways through the Forest, over many lifetimes.

Parents: We will.

> *The parents might now like to say or read anything they have prepared for their child.*

Druid: In the presence of the Lord and the Lady, we bless this child. May they live long and happy lives in the Light.

> *The circle is closed in the appropriate way.*

AGE OF CHOICE

Of all the rites of passage in this book, this is the most difficult to define and the only one that does not mark an easily pinpointed event. That does not make it any less important than any of the others. It is a highly significant transition.

The difficulty of defining the Age of Choice and deciding when it has been attained lies in the fact that it is dependent on the development of the person involved. As a simple guide, however, we can say that a person who is, on the whole, capable of being responsible for their lives and all its actions is someone who has attained the Age of Choice. That is, we are confident in their ability to make choices about relationships, spiritual matters, education, and so on because they are socially, psychologically, and spiritually aware of their place in the world.

This is a huge attainment, and it is only right that it is celebrated. However, we have to be aware that we are marking the *beginning* of the transition from childhood to adulthood. A young person may have reached the stage where they are capable of making decisions and being responsible for the consequences, but that does not mean the whole weight of independent living can be placed on their shoulders. They still have much to learn and much to experience.

There are so many factors involved, it is clear that the attainment of the Age of Choice will differ from person to person. And even where we might be reluctant to allow a person completely independent living, we can still mark their transition within the parameters of their own understanding of the world. The announcement that someone has attained this level of maturity must, therefore, be made by those who know the person well, *including* the person themselves. External or largely objective parameters are useless.

We are familiar with the fact that the law permits certain activities and decisions to be made by an individual when they reach specific ages. However, such standards pay little heed to the individuals to whom they are applied. In ancestral Celtic society, the Age of Choice was nominally set at 14, but that could be deferred if the individual involved was not considered capable. Surviving for a set number of years is simply no guide to how responsible a person may be.

The same is true of biological changes. Reaching sexual maturity is no indicator of whether a person has reached any other sort of maturity. In fact, the onset of puberty tends to have the opposite effect. Teenagers awash with hormones are not always able to behave responsibly. Add to this the fact that puberty is occurring at an increasingly earlier age and the consequences of using a biological marker are clear. The Age of Choice would be a declaration of sexual maturity and nothing else. For all sorts of reasons this is highly inappropriate.

This does not mean that our children should not know what sexual development entails. The more they know and understand about such things the more responsible they are likely to be. However, we should not be making a ceremony of our children's sexuality. Quite apart from the fact that you might receive a visit from the police, your children would probably never forgive you the trauma involved in being so paraded.

So how do we decide when a young person has reached the Age of Choice? Without wishing to sound like we are avoiding the question, all we can say is that you will know. Moreover, the better you get on with your children, the easier it will be. Be assured, however, it is not a test that requires a certain pass mark, any more than it is a magical transformation that occurs on a person's sixteenth birthday. No one becomes an adult in one go (no matter what life may do to them), and we all have lapses – although those who are allowed to be children and allowed to develop at their own pace often become more fully adult than do others. Be open to your child and let the Goddess guide you.

Preparation
Life is embarrassing enough for youngsters as it is, so keep this as simple and as informal as possible. It is a party for family and friends that begins with a short ceremony.

The Ritual

The Druid presiding can be a guest for the celebration, a parent, or friend. There need not be a circle, but if the young person on whose behalf the ritual is being performed consents, it adds to the importance of the event. The young person should sit in the middle.

Druid: We have come to this place on the [*day, month, and year*] to welcome [*young person's name*] to adulthood.

(*to young person*) Your mother and father, family and friends have all supported and cared for you this far on your journey through life. Now has come the time to honour that support and care, for as you become an adult, you will now need to offer care and support in your turn. This is the never-ending cycle of ancestors, weaving a golden thread through our lives from birth to death and through to birth again. As you honour your ancestors, so they honour and care for you on the path the Goddess has chosen for you to tread this time. We ask the Goddess and God to empower you, on this, *your* journey.

The Druid lifts a chalice containing mead. They give some to the Land, some to the Goddess, and then pass the chalice to the young person.

Great Goddess we ask you to watch over and ever guide [*young person's name*]

The young person drinks from the goblet. It is then passed back to the Druid, who walks the circle asking each person present to drink in the young person's honour. The Druid then walks the circle again, this time with the participant, and the guests greet, hug, kiss, or give gifts for which the young person gives thanks. If the young person so wishes, they can then read a poem or other suitable piece. When all this is done, the Druid returns to the centre.

In the name of the Great Goddess, you now take the first steps from being a child to being an adult. May you be blessed with the cauldron's gifts. May you live in the Light.

There should now follow a family feast with the opening of presents.

INDEPENDENCE (House Blessing)

Independence comes in many forms and at many levels. We learn to walk and talk, we go to school, make friends... However, none is more resonant than the day we branch out and leave the family home to set up on our own. It marks the moment when the transition from childhood to adulthood is complete.

The druidic pun above is intentional as independence is relative. No matter how much we may flourish and fruit as a branch in our own right, we cannot sever ourselves from our roots. They made us. And even if we labour the analogy and consider ourselves instead to be fruit of the vine or seed of the flower, our form is still that of the parent. We should not deny that, no matter how much we may find that to be distasteful.

However, being conscious of where we came from does not mean that we cannot decide where we wish to go. That is, after all, one of the reasons for independent living. It is a renewal, a fresh chance, an opportunity to enhance the life of the world, your communities (new and old), and your self.

Independence is, quite literally, vital. Dependency, especially on a childhood expectancy of family, means reliance on something that quite naturally fades and dies. If we are not capable of independent life (no matter that we might look after our parents in their old age), we will wither before our due time and our potential as a force in the world will not be realized.

It is equally vital that we retain contact with our roots for they help to feed us. The strength of the tree is in its ability to remain anchored whilst it reaches outward to the air and sunlight. In our own case as beings striving for independence this is important to remember. What we embark upon has been done before. By staying in touch with the place we have come from, we can learn from all the mistakes and triumphs of those who have gone before us and apply them to our own unique situation.

This is even more important today as society offers us far fewer forms of support than were available in times past. We may have greater scope for independence, but it is at the cost of widely scattered communities with ever more fragile lines of communication. Most of us cope with this remarkably well, but all the same, for many it can be a fearful and very lonely time.

If you do have problems adjusting, do not be afraid to get help. This is easier said than done. There are not always places to go or people to whom you can turn. In addition, those most likely to have problems are also those who find it difficult to approach others. However, there is no shame in admitting you are not coping well and it is far better to do it sooner than later, when the problems are small and surmountable. If you are at college or university, there should be someone whose job it is to help. If you are striking out on your own, arrange your own support. Keep in touch with family and friends on a regular basis. They will understand.

That is why we advocate establishing an altar, even if you are in just the one, small room. This will be your spiritual centre, a token of the hearth you have left, and your link with your ancestors (including the still living ones). It is a centre of calm in what is likely to be, to begin with, a hectic and confusing world. If you have a serene and steady centre in place, blessed by the Goddess, you can better face the new world into which you are emerging.

Preparation
This is not a big ritual, but it does require that you clean your new home (physically and spiritually) and then establish a hearth or altar. That means you need to set aside an appropriate amount of time and ensure you have all the bits and pieces you need. Your hearth or altar needs to be a safe place to burn candles. This can be adapted for couples moving in together.

For the ceremony, you will need:
- A candle in a holder or lantern.
- Eight or more smallish stones.
- Rosemary (either fresh or dried).

Finish off with a simple, celebratory meal.

The Ritual

Start this ritual, as far as is practicable, by physically cleaning the whole of your new home. Open the windows and let the fresh air blow through, wash down all surfaces, beat rugs, wash curtains, and generally spruce the place up. You might also like to place fresh flowers or dried herbs in various rooms as you go. Allow the appropriate amount of time – a house may take days.

This may not feel much like a ritual at this stage, but all this activity will allow you to claim the space as your own as you clear away the spiritual vibrations of the previous occupants. It is also much easier to do all this when you first move in before you start unpacking and getting settled. Try to do any cleaning during daylight hours with the ritual proper performed in the evening of a full or waxing moon.

Whilst you are cleaning, choose a suitable location for your altar. Pick a spot where it will be safe to light candles and burn incense. Try also to make a place that is private as far as the layout of your new home will allow.

Before you start the rite, have a bath or shower and prepare yourself with some meditation for a few minutes. Feel clean and fresh.

You will not be casting a circle, as you will need to move freely about the house. Begin by sitting with your unlit candle in front of your altar. Have with you the rosemary and a dish containing the stones. Draw your new home about you, aware of the space you have cleansed and made your own. When you are ready, stand and say:

At home with one's self, I light this candle.

Light the candle.

I cleanse this house of the old.

Carrying the candle, walk through each of the rooms, or around the room if you are in a bedsit. Place a sprig or a pinch of rosemary in each of the rooms or at the window and door. As you go, say:

Goddess, I ask:
A blessing upon this new home,
A blessing upon this new hearth,
A blessing upon this new dwelling.

By this newly kindled fire, I ask:
A blessing upon each room,
A blessing upon all that is done within,
A blessing upon all that help.

[By this flame, I ask:
A blessing upon the garden,
A blessing upon all its fruits,
A blessing upon all its creatures.]

By your love, I ask:
A blessing upon all my kith and kin,
A blessing upon all my companions,
A blessing upon myself.

May wisdom and compassion guide me.
Be this blessing upon me
In the light and darkness,
Each day and night of my life.

Return to the altar.

In this space, I now grow into my independence. This is a true transition from child to adult.

Goddess, watch over this house and watch over me. May only peace, love, health, and joy enter this place.

Be seated once more. Place your candle in a safe place. Take the stones and, using your intuition, create a stone circle with them on the floor. In your own words, ask the quarters to empower them to keep you and your new home safe. The stones can then be placed where you want them around the house for added protection - one in each room or in groups. Leave the rosemary for a few days before spreading it in the garden or a nearby green space.

BINDING (Handfasting)

We bind ourselves to many people, groups, and organizations during our life. Most of these connections do not need to be marked in any special way. Some are marked by the special nature of the relationship itself. Just occasionally, we feel the need to make a formal statement. Where this involves a private commitment, those involved can create a small binding ceremony of their own, appropriate to the situation. More formal bindings that require public recognition are another matter.

Pledging to spend the rest of your life with another person is an enormous commitment. A partnership of this nature requires a great deal of confidence and maturity on the part of those involved. It also requires a high degree of independence. This may seem to be a paradox, but it is important lest one person becomes subsumed within the other.

Our personalities develop through our relationships with others, especially those we spend most time with and to whom we are closest emotionally and spiritually. We often complete our development as persons through the life-partner to whom we are attracted.

Pledging to a partner is also a sign that we have recognized we are a social being that requires companionship – someone with whom we can share everything. This does not suit everyone and we should feel no shame if we prefer to be alone. We are simply on a different track this time round.

Sadly, there is enormous social pressure to conform to some vague notion of 'marriage' that has often, over the centuries, been an institution of repression. The same is true with regard to children. There is far too much pressure on couples in general and women in particular to have children – with the insinuation that they are somehow lacking if they do not have them. In all this, we must come to know ourselves fully and be true to what we are as well as open with each other.

How our ancestors organized the marriage ceremony and what vows they took are unknown to us. We do know a great deal about the law as it relates to marriage and we also know that trial marriages were not only allowed, but also that they were probably commonplace. As there were legal implications in both cases, it is certain that a Druid would have been present to witness the union, if not actually presiding.

117

Trial unions were probably witnessed at one of the ceremonies of the eightfold year with a promise by the couple to stay together for a year and a day. It can be supposed that most trial marriages became permanent, but they were a civilized way of allowing a couple to find out whether they were suited to a life together whilst also allowing them the legal protection afforded permanently married couples.

Couples who wish to find out if they are compatible in this way now simply live together as society does not, in general, frown upon such arrangements - although they do not have the same legal rights as formally married couples. If a couple wishes to commit themselves for a year and a day, it would seem to be a much more personal arrangement these days and they should perhaps make their vows in a private ceremony.

When it comes to a lifetime commitment, we have become so used to the Christian ceremony that it is difficult to disassociate ourselves from its form, content, and symbolism. In particular, these ceremonies reflect the somewhat barbaric notion that unmarried women are the property of their father. The Christian ceremony (as so many others) is a transfer of property rights in the woman to the husband. If the bride feels that she wants to be presented then it is far more appropriate for the mother (as a representative of the Goddess) to do this.

The Handfasting we present below has no grounding in the past. It is an invention based on what we understand of past custom and can be changed to suit the taste of those being married. Although we have set it out as a ceremony for a heterosexual couple it will, with a little editing, work just as well for same-sex couples.

There is no jumping of broomsticks or binding with cords as these are borrowed from Eastern and African American practice. They have no basis in ancestral Celtic practice as far as we are aware. All we offer, in best Celtic tradition, is a simple and dignified means by which two people can declare their love and commitment before witnesses of their own choosing in a place consecrated by the presence of the Goddess.

Preparation

The detailed preparations for such an event must be left to those involved, as the ritual will form only a small part of the day. There are, however, a number of things that must be taken into consideration.

Remember, Handfasting is not legally binding. If you wish to be legally married, you must undertake a civil ceremony as well. Whether you do this on the same day or not is up to you, but it does add a whole extra dimension of things to organize and worry about – no matter how simple you may keep it. Remember, however, that some of your guests will want to be present at both ceremonies and having them on the same day may be a necessity.

Organizing everyone at ceremonies where large numbers of people attend is difficult. Simplicity is the best way. You do not want a highly choreographed ritual to go wrong on such an important day. Arrange for a rehearsal so that the principles know what is going to happen and where they should be.

Joyful as the occasion may be, the ritual itself is a solemn event. It also takes place within a sacred circle. No matter what children are allowed to do during the rest of the day, impress upon them how important the ceremony is, and ask them to be quiet and still for the few minutes that it takes.

Having your ceremony outside in a wood, glade, or garden is wonderful, but do remember you may be interrupted and that guests have to get to the site and then back to the nuptial feast. Seats are essential. Many of the guests will be in their best clothes, some will be elderly or infirm, and few of them will be used to sitting on the ground. It is also essential to have an alternative indoor venue, as you cannot rely on the weather – even with Druids presiding!

The couple who are marrying are expected to exchange vows and make declarations. This can be extremely nerve-wracking, especially as it is done in front of witnesses. Our advice, as ever, is to keep them simple and short. That way there is less likelihood of forgetting them or getting them wrong. It is far better to learn these by heart, but write them down as well and give them to the presiding Druid. Find a calligrapher to write them out for you or use a fancy font on a computer so that they look special. They can then be placed on the small table at the centre of the circle and referred to if necessary.

Music may be an important element to the ceremony. Entering and leaving the circle can certainly be accompanied by stately harp music, and you will no doubt want music during the feast. If you know any musicians, then live music is certainly a bonus, but recorded music will do just as well. Remember to test this all out at your chosen venue.

Make sure the bread offered during the ceremony is soft and white. Crusty bread, or anything decorated with grain or seed may cause choking – not what you want in the middle of the ritual. Keep some water on hand just in case.

Everyone will expect a cake at the feast afterwards, even though the wedding cake as we know it is a Victorian innovation - with the top layer being kept for the christening of the first child! A more agreeable option would be a large cake decorated with oak leaves, Celtic knotwork, or other appropriate designs.

For this ceremony, you will need:
- Mead in a flagon.
- A goblet from which to drink.
- Fresh bread on a platter.
- Rings or other tokens to be exchanged.
- Vows and declarations.
- A small table for the above.
- Music.

The ritual that follows is given with a full opening and closing as these differ slightly from those given earlier in the book.

The Ritual

Prepare a circle (or circles) of chairs for the guests with gaps at the quarters. Ensure the gap in the west is wide enough for the wedding party to approach the inner circle in comfort. Make sure the inner circle is large enough for the ceremony with the small table at the very centre. The burning incense in the south of the circle and the water in the west should be on sturdy stands. The items on the central table should be covered with a cloth.

When the guests are seated, the Druid presiding enters the space in the centre from the west followed by the couple and any attendants. All walk a complete circuit deiseal. The Druid stays in the west whilst the couple move to the centre, facing east with their attendants arrayed behind them. The Druid then walks deiseal to the east, salutes the quarter silently, walks a full circle back to the east, and turns outwards.

Druid: Oh, Great Goddess, I ask for your blessing, guidance, and protection on this handfasting ritual.

> *The circle is cast from east to east so that the guests are on the outside. The Druid walks to the south and takes the incense round the circle. They then walk to the west and do the same with the water, returning thereafter to the east. After a pause, they walk to the north and turn outwards. As they salute the quarter, they say:*

May there be peace in the North.

> *They walk to the south and turn outwards. As they salute the quarter, they say:*

May there be peace in the South.

> *They walk to the west and turn outwards. As they salute the quarter, they say:*

May there be peace in the West.

> *They walk to the east and turn outwards. As they salute the quarter, they say:*

121

May there be peace in the East.

They turn to face the centre and say:

May there be peace above and peace below. May there be peace throughout the worlds.

They say the prayer:

May we be blessed with the cauldron's gift,
May the breath of inspiration touch us,
May our voices always sing,
May the light reach within us,
May we learn from the Land,
May the seeds we plant be fruit for all children,
May calm be our mantle,
May wisdom blaze out from the depths of our souls,
May truth be in our hearts.

They say the Invocations:

O Great Goddess,
Bringer of life,
Queen of the Stars,
Mother of the Earth and Seas,
Be present now within this place.

O Great God,
Lord of the Land,
Guardian of the Wild Wood,
Walker of the silent ways,
Be present now within this place.

They turn outwards and say:

In the name of the spirit of Hawk, the springtime breeze, and the element of Air, I open this eastern gateway.

They walk to the south, turn outwards, and say:

In the name of the spirit of Adder, the power of the Sun, and the element of Fire, I open this southern gateway.

They walk to the west, turn outwards, and say:

In the name of the spirit of the Sacred Salmon, mighty oceans, and the element of Water, I open this western gateway.

They walk to the north, turn outwards, and say:

In the name of the spirit of Wolf, of dark, deep forests, and the element of Earth, I open this northern gateway.

They walk to the east, turn inwards, and say:

Welcome all. With the blessing of the Land, Sea, and Sky, I declare the opening of this handfasting ceremony within this sacred circle

They walk to the centre and face the couple across the table, uncovering the items there.

In sight of the Goddess, of the ancestors, and of the spiritual community of Druids, we here present have come together both to witness and to celebrate the union of [*bride's name*] and [*groom's name*].

Handfasting is a deep bond between two souls, equals drawn to journey together. As [*bride's name*] and [*groom's name*] go through this life they will experience many cycles of trial and triumph and much that is mundane. With the support and love of one another, their union will grow in strength, their hearts as one.

It is not within the Druid tradition to give a woman away, as a woman is no one's property. I do ask however that she has come here of her own free will to be handfasted this day.

Bride: *Affirms this in her own words.*

Druid: I also ask of the groom. Do you come here of your own free will to be handfasted this day?

Groom: *Affirms this in his own words.*

Druid: Then with the blessing of the Great Goddess, the twelve winds, and the Sacred Grove, let us hear the words and declarations you have prepared for each other.

The Bride hands any flowers to an attendant or places them on the table. Taking the hands of her loved one, she makes any vows and declarations that she has prepared. When she has finished, the Groom does the same.

Druid: May the love you have spoken of today encircle you both for ever, strengthen you, and protect you. May your love be as light as air, as deep as the greatest ocean, as strong as mountains, and as bright as the noonday sun.

Before you are bound together as the stones beneath you and the stars above, I must ask once again: Do you each come of your own free will? For yours alone is the right to bind yourself to another.

Both: We do. We wish to be bound together by our love.

Druid: [*bride's name*], it is your freely declared wish to bind [*groom's name*] to you. Place the ring on his finger as a token of this binding.

She places the ring on his finger.

Druid: [*groom's name*], it is your freely declared wish to bind [*bride's name*] to you. Place the ring on her finger as a token of this binding.

He places the ring on her finger.

Druid: As our ancestors once did, we will honour the Goddess this day with mead and bread.

The Druid pours mead from the flagon into the goblet, which he then hands to the bride. The bride pours a libation to the Land and then passes the goblet to the groom. He drinks, holds the goblet to the Sky, and then hands the goblet to the bride. She drinks and hands the goblet back to the Druid.

The Druid offers the bread on the platter to the groom. He picks up the bread, breaks off a piece for the Land, before handing it to the bride. The bride holds it to the Sky before breaking off a small piece to eat. She then hands the bread back to the groom who breaks off a small piece to eat before returning it to the Druid.

Druid: Having declared your love and commitment towards each other by this handfasting, I ask the Great Goddess to stand vigil over you both from this time hence. I ask that you be given everlasting love and wisdom, that you respect and cherish one another, whatever life puts in your way. With the blessing of your family, friends, and the ancestors, you have accepted eternal love in the sight of the Goddess. Two have become one. Your new lives are bound together. Blessed Be.

Bride and Groom kiss to seal the ceremony.

I declare that our work is done within this circle this day. May it be held in your memories and your hearts.

The Druid walks to the north, turns outwards, and says:

Spirits of the midnight cold, of crystal, and stones, I thank the element of Earth and close this northern gateway.

The Druid walks to the west, turns outwards, and says:

Spirits of evening light, of sacred spring and well, I thank the element of Water and close this western gateway.

The Druid walks to the south, turns outwards, and says:

Spirits of the Sun at noon, of mighty oak, and the sacred flame, I thank the element of Fire and close this southern gateway.

The Druid walks to the east, turns outwards, and says:

Spirits of the dawn, of lofty hill, and mighty gales, I thank the element of Air and close this eastern gateway.

The Druid faces the centre and says:

I thank the Goddess and the God, and all those seen and unseen who have joined this circle today.

Depart in peace. Hail and Farewell.

The Druid presiding waits until they are certain that all those who joined the circle from other worlds have departed.

I declare this handfasting ritual is now ended. It ends in peace, as in peace it began.

The Druid closes the circle tuathal, grounding it back into the Earth and up to the stars. When they reach the east again, they turn outwards and salute it in silence, before walking deiseal to the west.

The bride and groom then step back from the centre to the west and walk deiseal round the circle, followed by their attendants. They pause to salute the east, before leaving the circle in the west where the guests can greet them. The Druid waits until all have left before dismantling the table and its contents.

UNBINDING

All things come to an end. All cycles return us to the beginning, the point we were before we began. Some endings are expected, we can see them coming, perhaps even knew when they would occur from the very start. Others catch us unaware.

Of all these smaller cycles that run through the great cycles of our lives, it is the end of those in which we become emotionally engaged that cause us the greatest problems. Leaving school or college, moving from one job or home to another, the break-up of a personal relationship, illness, accident, death – all cause emotional turmoil, even if the end of the cycle is something we very much desire.

Every time such a cycle ends, we find that our psychological make-up is no longer adequate to cope, no longer sustainable. All the things that kept us going are no longer relevant or available and all the strategies we had developed for moving through life and coping with its vicissitudes are redundant. We are lost. If the cycle ends unexpectedly or in traumatic fashion, we are also left nursing psychological wounds.

For our own peace of mind, for healing, and to maintain a spiritual balance, we need, in private, to mark the end of important cycles in our life. Just as with casting a circle for rituals, we need to close them properly otherwise things never quite end.

Many of these important cycles are marked outwardly, but we must not neglect our inner life, especially at such sensitive times. If we do not take the time to close these circles on an inner plane, our emotions remain ragged, a hindrance to our forward path. The bonds must be properly disengaged otherwise we are forever looking in the wrong direction, weighed down by a past from which we cannot properly move away.

This is not to say that we should discard our past and the legacy of our emotional involvements. Far from it. They are what make us, shape our personality, colour our response to other people and to events. However, to try to cling to emotional attachments that have come to the end of their life is to stunt the development of our self and, especially in the case of those who have died, it is to hold back the spiritual development of others.

When a cycle has finished, we have to acknowledge that it has finished. We have to close that circle, cherish all that was good about it, seek out lessons that we might learn from it (but not too analytically as that can also prevent us from moving on as we mawkishly pick over the bones of the past), accept that it has changed us, celebrate that, and then move on.

After all, the end of one cycle is the beginning of another. We cannot do justice to the now and to the new if we are still entangled with the old, or if our emotional ghosts still haunt us.

Preparation

This is likely to be a highly charged ritual in which, at times, you may be vulnerable. Always do this inside, even if you wish, as part of the process, to visit a grave or some other place. Save that until afterwards when your soul has had time to start healing.

The ritual given below is for the unbinding of two people, but with a few small changes it can be applied to other situations, such as leaving school or college (always an emotional wrench), or the death of a loved one (and despite attending other ceremonies we all need to let go at a very personal level as well).

Take your time and do not expect instant results. This is an act of healing. You start the process here. It may take some time to complete. However, the healing will never occur unless you do make a start.

When you have finished, take a bath or shower and then sit down to a simple meal, allowing yourself to ground and return to the world slowly.

For the ceremony, you will need:
- A candle.
- Possibly mementos and photographs on which to meditate, depending on the nature of the unbinding.

The Ritual

Create a safe and sacred space by walking a circle three times. Start in the west and salute the east. You may feel you want to use the full solo opening and closing.

When the circle is complete, stand in the centre and light the candle. Close your eyes and follow your breath for a few heartbeats. Relax into yourself. Take all the time you need. This type of working can bring up many feelings and emotions that may be stressful. When you are ready, read the following words (or other more relevant ones that you have prepared) very softly and gently, either out loud or inwardly.

I have come into this sacred space at this time to release myself from bonds that no longer hold true.

The bonds were between me and [*name of person/place*].

I hold no anger.

I release all negative memories.

I will hold close only the memories of our friendship and the love that once we shared.

Take a few moments to let the words spoken enter your heart.

I ask the Goddess to witness this unbinding of two souls, and ask that we both be blessed and healed as we walk our separate ways once more.

Sit now and meditate.

Follow your breath and as you do, release all the fears, anger, resentments, and sadness as you breathe out.

Now see yourself and the other person together. Bind a blue circle of light and love around yourself and around the other person (or some symbol of that from which you are now parted), in the form of a figure of eight. Where the circles join between you, break the bond by melting it apart. You will then each have a circle of protection around you to help you get through the weeks ahead. The circles will gradually fade and with them will go all the hurts, confusions, and pain.

When this is done and you feel ready, stand, walk to the south, and face outwards.

I ask the powers of the South to warm our hearts once more.

Walk to the west and face outwards.

I ask the powers of the West to allow the waters of healing to flow around us.

Walk to the north and face outwards.

I ask the powers of the North to ground us both as we start to grow again as individuals.

Walk to the east and face outwards.

I ask the powers of the East to allow the winds of change and time to bring clarity in our new lives.

Pause for a moment and allow yourself to accept the reality of the unbinding.

This unbinding is now complete. From this moment starts a new cycle in my life. As I close this circle may its light radiate out into the world.

When you are ready, close your circle in the appropriate way. Visualize both love and light spreading out across the universe.

DEATH

Death is not an end any more than it is an isolated event. It is an integral part of the process that is our life. If we do not die, we cannot have lived. And having lived, we complete but one small part of a much larger cycle. The more abstract aspects of this are considered in the next section. Here, we are concerned with the practicalities of solemnizing an event in the existence of someone we hold dear.

We are rarely present at the moment of death of a loved one. The pressure of our own lives and the way in which health care is organized (along with strong anecdotal evidence that many people who are dying actually hold on until their loved ones have left them alone) often prevent us from keeping vigil. This may be a cause for regret, but it is not something about which we should feel in the wrong. Our ways are parting and it is right that the living should continue to live.

At the same time, we are all aware that someone who is dying derives great solace from the presence of those they know and care for. The secret is to remember that what is happening, no matter how distressing the circumstances or premature the event, is part of the natural order. We are helping someone at a difficult time. We do it in other ways without demur. Helping a person as they leave this world should be no different. We should not be scared by death and we should make every effort to be with our loved one when they need us most.

It is also important to remember that a person who is dying is not passive. They participate. It is their transition, after all. We cannot stop what is happening, but we should be there to offer our love, companionship, and support. It can be as simple as holding someone's hand and telling them you love them. It also involves respecting their wishes. They rely on us at a time when they are, in most respects, helpless.

Those who have been through this know how disorientating it can be for all involved, how time and reality take a holiday. We become so absorbed in this very small part of the world that emerging from hospital after a visit is like stepping on to another planet. When death comes, no matter how prepared we may feel, it is always a shock. We are left numbed by events as well as assailed and confused by our emotions – particularly if the person who has died went through a great deal of suffering. And whilst it is natural that such emotional turmoil causes us to focus on our self, we should not forget whom this is all about.

The ritual, short as it is, is a potent reminder of this. It restores a much-needed sense of balance in our lives at a time of extremes. It also reminds us that the cause of our grief will be a cause of joy in the Otherworld where the soul of the departed will be reborn. We have every right to mourn, to express our sense of loss, but our loved one is moving on to a place that is as much a part of our reality as the place in which you read this.

At a more mundane level, the ritual gives us something to do at a time when there is nothing left to do, at a time we feel most helpless – especially if we were present at the moment of death. It is a formal, yet gentle goodbye (and we can say our informal goodbyes with an Unbinding ritual), an acknowledgement that our ways have now parted.

It also grounds us. Although it speaks of the departed soul, of their rest and their re-awakening, it also speaks to us who remain of a new cycle in our lives. We must now return to the world we know and come to terms with its new shape.

Preparation
There is very little you can or should do to prepare for this ritual. Circumstances dictate against that. It is deliberately simple and short so that it can be performed anywhere and at any time.

You will need to obtain permission to light a candle if the ceremony takes place in a hospital, hospice, or nursing home. Do not be surprised if the relevant authorities are reluctant to allow this. They have to consider fire regulations and the very real risk posed to others. Explain that it is important to you and to the departed, but do not get upset about it if they refuse. It is not important in the scheme of things and you can always light a candle at home if you feel the need.

If you are allowed to light a candle, remember to keep one with you (along with a safe stand and a means of lighting it) at all times.

The Ritual

This ritual is performed as soon after death as possible (never before). Do not cast a circle, as this would inhibit the passing of the soul from this world to the next. The person making the invocation and blessing should, as far as is practicable, stand to the west of the deceased.

Our loss is the Otherworld's gain.
They share our sorrow as we share their joy.

Goddess and God, be with us at this time of transition. We ask that with your blessings, the sailing to the Blessed Isles in the farthest West is a safe and smooth journey for [*name of deceased and any magical names if known*].

Light a candle.

You go home this day,
To your home of winter,
To your home of autumn,
Of spring and of summer.
You go home this day to your lasting home,
To your rest of great deserving,
To your sound sleeping,
To a new dawn
And a new day.

All those present should say goodbye in whatever way feels right. When they have finished, extinguish the candle and leave quietly.

FUNERAL

In the immediate aftermath of death, we have neither the time nor the inclination for more than a short ritual to ask for a blessing on the departed one and their forthcoming journey. We say our first goodbye and make a start on closing the circle of our relationship. We then need a moment for ourselves, a moment to rest and to start our own healing. Part of this may be a personal Unbinding ritual where we can deal with issues and memories that we do not want to share. We must then complete our engagement with the passing of our loved one and re-enter the world. This is accomplished through the funeral rites.

Modern attitudes to parting, death, and the funeral have become extremely morbid – a legacy of Victorian times. For all their protestation of Christian values and beliefs, the prevalent view of the world was (and still is) materialistic. Ancestral Celts, however, knew without any doubt that the universe is a realm of both matter and spirit, each invested in the other. For them, the sadness of losing a loved one was much tempered by knowing they had a new life ahead of them. There would be no dwelling on the cold clay of the grave, no mawkish revelling in grief. Instead, they would celebrate the life just gone, along with the promise of the new one to come.

A wake would be held as a mark of respect, lasting from the moment of death until the disposal of the remains. This was a mixture of solemn vigil, quiet contemplation, a recounting of the life of the departed one, and feasting. Such an approach to death would enable the wider community to participate, offering their condolences, and adding their own perspective to the memory of the departed. The sharing of reminiscences allowed a much fuller picture to emerge, even in a society where tribal groups were small and everyone knew everyone else. Telling the tales affirmed the life.

The communal aspect of mourning was and is important for another reason. As we have already noted (and as anyone who has experienced this knows), the death of someone close causes us to withdraw from the everyday world. A funeral or memorial is a means of returning to the world, easing the transition, helping in the healing process, and mirroring the journey of the departed one.

It also provides energy and comfort for the days to come when we are faced with the task of sorting out legacies and belongings and finding that everyday life is different, that things we once did can no longer be done or shared.

Preparation

We have written the following ritual so that it can be used at a burial or cremation, or as a memorial service. Circumstances may be that the family of the deceased want a private ceremony of their own. To avoid confusion at your own funeral, plan it yourself and stipulate what you want in your will or some other document signed and witnessed by others.

Part of the funeral process must, with a Druid, include the disposal of anything that was used by them for ritual purposes or which was closely associated with their spiritual activity. Wands, chalices, talismans – none of these should be passed on to others. They should be buried or cremated with the body if possible; otherwise, a separate ceremony may be necessary. You will need to discuss this with whoever is carrying out the funeral. This is worth bearing in mind when choosing your own ritual paraphernalia – make sure they are made of natural materials.

You can, of course, conduct the entire funeral yourself as long as you have the required permissions for the site of burial, scattering of ashes, planting of trees, and whatever else may be required. There are also a number of professional funeral directors who now organize pagan and green funerals.

Finish with a feast. Everyone will need the opportunity to ground themselves and to talk. After all, funerals are one of the few times these days that families gather. Keep the whole thing informal for by this stage, the time for rituals is over.

The Ritual

As the mourners arrive, music appropriate to the occasion and dear to the departed one can be played. Carrying a sprig or wand of yew, the Druid presiding waits until all present are settled. They should not cast a circle as the soul of the departed needs free passage. However, they can enclose those gathered with a protective and healing light.

We have gathered today to bestow our love and blessings on our dear brother/sister [*deceased's name*], for they have started on their journey to the sacred place our Druid ancestors called the Blessed Isles. We ask in the name of the Great Goddess that the journey be both swift and smooth.

We are, of course, saddened by the departure of [*deceased's name*] who [*brief acknowledgement of how they died*]. However, as Druids we know in our hearts that whilst death may be the end of one life, it also the beginning of another in the never-ending cycle of birth, life, death, and rebirth within the divine cauldron.

In our sorrow, it is hard for us to understand this. Indeed, it may take many moons before our sorrow is replaced by good and happy memories of our loved one. The healing begins today. And as the departed one takes their first steps into a new world, so must we take our first steps back into this, allowing them their new life as they have allowed us ours.

[*Deceased's name*],
In care of the Goddess,
You go home this day,
To your home of winter,
To your home of autumn,
Of spring and of summer.
You go home this day to your lasting home,
To your rest of great deserving,
To your sound sleeping,
To a new dawn,
And a new day.

Sleep now and so fade sorrow,
Sleep, [*deceased's name*], in the heart of truth.

Be the sleep of seven lights upon you,
Be the sleep of seven joys upon you,
Be the sleep of seven slumbers upon you.

Sleep in the quiet of quietness,
Sleep in the way of guidance,
Sleep in the heart of love,
Sleep, [*deceased's name*], everlasting in our hearts.

To wake,
In a new light,
In a new love,
In a new life.

Pause.

If anyone would like to say anything in celebration of the life of [*deceased's name*], please step forward.

Friends and family should now pay tribute. The Druid presiding may also read any passage or poem requested by the deceased.

At this point, the coffin is lowered into the grave, conveyed to the furnace, or the ashes are scattered. Music dear to the departed one should be played.

We now commend [*deceased's name*] to their new journey. At this parting of ways, may the Goddess bless us all and guide our steps.

The Druid presiding radiates healing and protective light out into the world. More gentle music plays, allowing people to sit in meditation before they leave. The Druid should remain on hand to offer comfort to the family of the bereaved and to ensure that the ceremony is properly completed and the site cleared.

PART THREE

THE SEA

THE PERSONAL

The eightfold year, we have seen, is a ritual manifestation of the Sky and is concerned with the world. Our rites of passage relate to the Land and are concerned with community. The final section of this book deals with what is, at one and the same time, the smallest and the largest of our spiritual concerns - the personal.

That one aspect is large and the other is small does not mean that one is more important than the other. It is merely a reflection of scope and of focus. One is the immediate and highly intimate concern of our everyday lives, and the other is the distant and vast unknown of the voyage that our spirits take on the death of our material selves.

These concerns are tied here by the element to which they both belong – the Sea. In the case of the cycle of life, death, and re-birth, it is quite literally the Sea as personified by the Western Ocean across which we all travel when our soul moves from this world to the Other. Yet vast as any sea may be, it is water, and water itself goes through a cycle that lends itself to the vast and to the small. From the ocean, water rises as vapour under the power of the Sun. It forms clouds (the fruit of the cycle) that eventually let fall rain. Each drop is a seed that will grow to become an ocean, ready to produce the fruit once more.

In each drop, each seed, is to be found the basis for the cycle that celebrates the self. This is not self-aggrandizement, but a simple acknowledgement in our daily life of our existence as beings integral to the world. Herein lies one of the great mysteries. For we lead humble existences, no matter what some of us may believe. We must eat, drink, earn a living, keep house, and do all those day-to-day things that keep body and soul together. Yet in this, especially if it is done in true and right fashion, is the very basis of a spiritual life. If we live simply and acknowledge our true being, live faithfully to that and our beliefs, each humble act of life becomes a prayer.

We can accentuate this with words to be said as we embark on these everyday things. Words said with feeling and with understanding. The mere rote repetition of formulae is of no use. Our words must engage us with the world and draw us in to ever-closer communion.

Striking up a conversation with what we do acts to make us pay attention to what it is we are doing and why we do it. So much is superfluous in our lives that we need to strip it away. Conversing in this manner makes it easier to see the simpler ways there are of walking in the world.

Within this simplicity and focus on the self, however, we will find the vastness of all existence and the great mystery of life, death, and rebirth - for these are also symbolized by the water, the great sea which is created by those small drops, those seeds, as they flow together in rivulets, streams, and rivers down to the shore where, finally, they feed the ocean.

This cycle is also an apt symbol of our lives. In material form, we consider ourselves as individuals. Yet for the most part, we are far too integrated with the rest of the world for this to have any absolute meaning. After all, how long does a raindrop remain a raindrop? Even as it falls from the clouds it will collide with others, merge, and reform.

Once the raindrop reaches the ground, it enters into a complex of cycles that help to sustain all life. This experience ineradicably alters the water and may engage it in many different cycles and relationships before it reaches a free-flowing stream that can start it on its final journey to the sea where identity is lost in the whole.

Yet that is not the end. Eventually, each molecule, each raindrop will rise to begin a new cycle – falling who knows where and following who knows what new and wonderful journey.

SMALL WATER

Celts, through the ages, have had a prayer and a blessing for every conceivable occasion. In fact, they have had many prayers for each occasion, and where they lacked one their nature was such that they could easily extemporize. With short rhymes and lengthy pieces, they invoked the gods, goddesses, and spirits to weave together the everyday world with the world of spirit.

Prayer is a constant act of renewal. Our ancestors knew (and we must relearn) that creation was not a far distant and one-off event. It is a continuous process in which we must play our part and for which we must accept our responsibilities. Getting that part right, acting correctly, and fulfilling our responsibilities toward the rest of creation is helped by constant appeal to those higher powers that are willing to help as long as we are willing to accept our place.

This should not be taken in a hierarchical sense. The concept of a chain of being does not accord with the way in which the real world works. Accepting our place means knowing where, in the vast web of life, we properly belong. It also means not doing things that would distort or cut the strands of the web. After all, if we disturb too many, our own sources of sustenance – both material and spiritual – will be denied us.

Everyday life is guided by the rhythm of the day and the month. These were the most obvious natural divisions of the flow of time and still shape the way in which we live, for all that we now have clocks, artificial lighting, and almost instantaneous communication. We evolved over millions of years to these rhythms and we do ourselves damage if we fight against them.

The general framework of life was the month. This is the dance of the Great Mother and reflects the cycle of both her fertility and that of all her daughters. Each month began when the moon was full, this being the easiest phase to identify visually. From this, we derive the other natural unit of time – the fortnight (fourteen nights). The seven-day week may be considered as natural, falling (more or less) on each of the lunar quarters, but it does not feature in ancestral timekeeping.

So, it is the full moon and the new moon that help to govern the shape of the everyday. In following a solar calendar, we all too easily lose touch with the rhythm of the moon. Our ancestors lived their lives quite naturally by this cycle. We must try to ensure that we do the same. A few moments each night should be given over to viewing the moon and becoming constantly aware of its phases and its position in the sky. There are good quality lunar calendars and diaries these days to help us become attuned.

This is not just a matter of being in tune with our ancestors, although this is no bad thing in itself. It also makes sense materially, psychologically, and spiritually. Materially, it tunes our physical body to one of the major cycles of our existence and with the one planetary body that has a significant effect on the earth and all life thereon. We tend, for example, to be more sexually active around the time of the full moon. Birth rates are, unsurprisingly, thought to peak in a similar cycle.

Psychologically, we are affected by the lunar cycle. Our bodies change with the phases of the Moon just as the seas do. Accidents, crimes, and irrational behaviour follow a lunar cycle, reaching their peaks around the time of the full moon – hence the term lunacy. Although this is largely a statistical effect to be discerned in large populations, it is recognized as a genuine phenomenon.

Spiritually, following the cycles of the moon is an important and ongoing link with the Goddess. Becoming aware of her cycles of fertility not only reflects how we act in everyday life, it brings us closer to the realities of the spiritual world. This is not some strange phantasmal dimension, although our experience of it may often stand our accepted notions of existence on their head. It is a reflection of the material world – hence our ancestors' belief that one of the main gates to the Otherworld was through still water.

Learning to look at and meditate on the Moon is a ritual activity in itself, encompassed within a general knowledge of the night sky. This is something for which our Druid ancestors were renowned and it is well worth cultivating in ourselves if for no other reason than that the night sky is so beautiful.

To acknowledge our link with the Goddess, and to help keep track of the true months, we offer here both a full moon ritual and a short, traditional blessing for the new moon.

ARIANRHOD'S DANCE – a Full Moon Ritual

The full Moon ritual is by no means just a female one. Men honour the Great Goddess as well, although this is often forgotten. Some feel shy of this, anxious about straying into the territory of 'women's mysteries'. There are none. The mysteries are open to all. The Great Mother does not discriminate against any of her children, any more than does the God.

This ritual is, of course, best performed outside. It can, however, be performed in a room from which the Moon is visible. If neither is possible then, weather permitting, try to get outside for a few minutes to see the moon and pay homage.

Preparation

For this ceremony, you will need a small, dark bowl filled with water. If you are working indoors, you may also want the following:

- Candles.
- Incense.
- Mead, wine, or fruit juice.
- A chalice.

The Ritual

When you are ready, perform the appropriate opening. After a brief pause, acknowledge the Moon and then walk deiseal to whichever part of the circle feels comfortable. This can change with each Moon, completing a full circle in each year. Alternatively, you may prefer to work from the centre.

This is the time of the Great Mother Goddess, when Arianrhod's Dance lights the night sky in greatest glory, when I feel the fullness of your power and the brightness of your love.

As I look up at the bright circle of the Goddess, I ask that you bless the animal, plant, and mineral kingdoms of the Earth upon which you shine, protecting all with your light.

Move to the bowl and try to can catch the reflection of the Moon in the water. Gaze on this for a while, and give your own blessings to the three kingdoms. Use your own words, spoken from the heart. Do not rush this. Take as long as you need.

I honour the Goddess at this time of full Moon, She who gives my life growth, nurturing, and love.

I honour the Goddess at this time of full Moon, She who rules the tides of the great waters, of sexuality, and dreams.

I honour the Goddess at this time of full Moon, She who gives me inspiration and intuition in the cycles of my life.

Walk your circle three times.

I invoke Arianrhod, She who is queen of Caer Sidi, the great spiral castle.

She stands dressed in starlight, holding the wondrous silver wheel of destiny and creativity.

In her glory, she dances across the skies, inspiring all who will listen to her wisdom.

She awakens the instinct in us as we listen without ears to her magic. She speaks to us within if we are still and prepared to hear.

Stand in the light of the Moon, if possible, raise your arms, and feel yourself absorbing its power.

The full Moon is a suitable time to make a divination or to bring things in your life to fruition. Scrying with the bowl of water is the most appropriate method at this time, but others with which you are more comfortable are just as acceptable.

When you have finished, thank the Goddess for the abundance in your life.

Stay in meditation for a while.

When you are ready, close your circle in the appropriate way.

NEW MOON

In some ways, the cycle of the Moon reflects the cycle of the year. The full Moon is akin to midsummer whilst the dark Moon is akin to midwinter. Small wonder that the new Moon – the first sight of the Moon after as many as three nights of darkness - was greeted with such joy. It is a return of light to the darkness, proof that the newborn had survived. The anthems that were sung have survived the millennia. Below is one such, collected by Alexander Carmichael, which retains its pagan feel. If you practice a regular full Moon ritual, you may also wish to build a short ceremony around this piece for the new Moon.

Queen of the night
Hail unto thee,
Jewel of the night!

Beauty of the heavens,
Jewel of the night!

Mother of the stars,
Jewel of the night!

Fosterling of the sun,
Jewel of the night!

Majesty of the stars,
Jewel of the night!

PRAYER/INVOCATION
As well as the cycles of the moon, our ancestors marked the turning of each day; especially as such a natural and obvious rhythm ruled their domestic activity. Sunrise, midday, and sunset would have been three key markers used in a time before the tyranny of the clock.

Notions of the eight tides of the day are a late introduction from non-Celtic sources. In itself, this does mean they are 'bad', but they do depend on clock time, which runs counter to the notion of natural rhythms and cycles that fluctuate in sympathy with the seasons. This is noticeable in the length of daylight hours when most work would have been done. When there is most to do outside, it is summer and the days are longer. As winter approaches, those things we need to do to sustain ourselves can be done mostly indoors.

Beyond that, the rhythms of the day would have been entirely personal – the ever evolving content of one's own life and relationships shaping the terms of one's own conversation with the immediately spiritual. In all that we do, our actions resonate through the worlds and have an effect there. In all that we do, we create - and if we do not, we should perhaps question why we do it at all. In acts of creation, in acts that affect the spiritual, we need guidance. That guidance comes from the constant conversation we conduct through the medium of our prayers, blessings, invocations, and anthems.

Each person in ancestral times, irrespective of what task they were engaged in, would have asked a blessing on their enterprise. Moreover, they would not have relied on words out of a book. Our ancestors were an eloquent people. They would have had personal prayers that, perhaps, were handed down from parent to child and teacher to apprentice, but they would also have engaged themselves by talking with the divine in everyday terms.

Some examples follow.

Ritual chant

To raise power prior to undertaking a ritual or some other task that requires both physical and spiritual strength.

Power of stone I give to thee,
Of fish and beast and bird,
Power of the seas, and power of the trees,
Of Moon and Stars and Earth.
Power of the Land,
Power of the Skies,
Power of above and below,
Power of the ancestors, and power of sight,
Power of the Sacred Grove.

General blessing

A short, general blessing is also a useful tool to have for those moments when you need words but in which the situation takes them from you.

Goddess preserve us,
Keep us from harm,
Hear me now,
And empower my charm.

Blessing of greeting
We might also wish to give a general blessing to people as a formal style of greeting during ritual and ceremony.

By the stones be thou grounded,
By the ocean be thou pure,
By the breeze be thou inspired,
By the flame be thou blessed.

Thanks for food
Although most often associated with Christian practice, giving thanks for the food on our plates is an essential of any pagan path. This is, after all, the closest link that many of us now have with the Land. And do not forget to thank the cook as well.

In this life given is my life,
In this life riven is my life,
Our thanks for this sacrifice.
Goddess bless this food,
Be it pure, be it wholesome,
Our thanks to the Land.

Blessing on a child/loved one going out
No matter how old our children, we worry about their health and their safety and although we do not want them to feel confined by what we do, gentle advice never does harm. Nor does the following blessing.

May the Goddess watch you
And return you safe to this hearth.
Be every season bright for thee,
Joy of night and day be thine,
Light of Sun and Moon be thine.
Walk a straight path,
Walk a safe path,
Belovéd of my heart.

Blessing on a loved one
Even those of us who are inseparable may face the possibility of a loved one having to travel away for a while. This can be hard and unsettling and a simple blessing can help ease the uncertainty we feel.

Be the Goddess by thy side,
To protect and to guide.
Be the spirit on thee.

Calming of the spirit
There are times when our spirit is in turmoil and we need a moment to allow it to calm. A simple chant can help as it allows us to focus on the task. This chant can also be used as a prelude to meditation.

Upon all things my senses reach,
Be there peace.
Upon all things beyond me,
Be there peace.

The peace of the western sea,
The peace of the distant isle,
The peace of the cloudless sky.

The peace of the forest,
The peace of the salmon pool,
The peace of the flower in bloom.

Peace on this body,
Peace on this soul,
Peace on this spirit.

Blessing on the self
Although we are inclined to think of others first, we should not neglect ourselves.

Goddess enfold me,
Goddess protect me,
Goddess in my words,
Goddess in my thoughts,
Goddess in my deeds.

On going to sleep

Sleep is a mysterious thing and can be daunting, especially for young ones. This prayer is for adults. Words for children can be composed on finding out what troubles them (if anything).

As I sink now into welcome sleep
Be it that the world's shadow brings both peace and healing,
Be it that those I love rest easy,
Be it that the Goddess watch over me,
Be it that my soul's work is just and lasting,
Be it that my troubles are resolved,
Be it that my dreams are restful and inspiring,
Be it that we all lie safe from hurt and harm.

On waking

Whatever we may have to face when we wake, we know that we do not face it alone. The following reminds us that the world is a blessing bestowed upon us by the Goddess, but its wording can also be taken as an invocation.

Each thing that I see,
The Goddess' blessing.
Each thing that I touch,
The Goddess' blessing.
Each sound that I hear,
The Goddess' blessing.
Each scent that I smell,
The Goddess' blessing.
Each thing that I taste,
The Goddess' blessing.
Each thought that guides me,
The Goddess' blessing.
Each act I complete,
The Goddess' blessing.
Strength this day,
Oh Goddess,
That I may be true, wise, and brave.

Protection for the family

There are times when we may feel uncertain about the safety of our loved ones and ourselves, or maybe discord has reached into the home. There may also be times (as any parent knows) when children have gone astray. At times such as this, a plea for protection can bring strength.

Power of three
To save,
To shield,
To surround
The hearth,
The home,
And those within.
This day,
This eve,
This night.

Blessing on an animal companion

Those of us who are lucky enough to be blessed with a companion animal know how precious their gift is to us. They bring comfort, friendship, healing, and joy into our lives. It is their selfless way of thanking us for food and shelter and love.

Lady of the Forest,
Goddess of all creatures,
Bless this friend,
That they be fleet,
And free of any care.

Lord of the Animals,
God of the Forest,
Bless this friend,
Keep them safe from harm,
Save them a place by the hearth.

On the washing of a baby
Children can seem so fragile, especially in the face of what they must encounter as they grow in this world of ours. Each time you bathe a child is an ideal opportunity to bless them with the gift of water and invoke good fortune as you care for them and cleanse them.

Nine small waves for thee,
Nine small blessings.

A small wave for your form,
A small wave for your eye,
A small wave for your hand,
A small wave for your voice,
A small wave for your health,
A small wave for your wisdom,
A small wave for your luck,
A small wave for your love,
A small wave for your soul.

Nine small waves for thee,
Nine small callings.
Nine small waves for thee,
Nine small blessings.

On taking a journey
All journeys, whether physical or spiritual, have their hazards and frustrations. Starting with a request for protection is always a good first step.

Goddess, I ask
A blessing on the path I take,
A blessing on all who travel.
See us safely there,
And safely home again.

Blessing for a spiritual journey

Bestowing a blessing on another is a small but important gift. It is a request for protection and strength, a request that whatever powers there may be watch over and guide the one who is blessed. This is especially apt for those who are about to undertake a spiritual journey or quest, no matter how small.

Wisdom of serpent be thine,
Wisdom of raven be thine,
Wisdom of nut-speckled salmon.

Strength of the Sea be thine,
Strength of the Land be thine,
Strength of boundless Sky.

Bounty of Sun be thine,
Bounty of Moon be thine,
Bounty of bright shining Stars.

Truth of word be thine,
Truth of thought be thine,
Truth of every deed.

Although we have provided some examples of the type and style of prayer or blessing that we mean, we encourage you to become familiar with the Celtic ethos and world view to the point that you can also extemporize. Working from the words of others is a good way to start, but it is important to keep the conversation alive and relevant by creating your own. Without that, it is easy to forget the need also to think carefully about that to which you are applying your prayer or blessing and why you are involved in a conversation about it in the first place.

Do not think that you have to be a poet to do this. A true spirit and a genuine desire to communicate will give quick, bright wings to your words and thoughts. Small water is spontaneous and without deliberate structure. It may develop structure as you find a form, but it will be entirely individual to you and your voice.

BIG WATER

The final voyage of this life is across the ocean in the West, following the setting Sun at the end of the day. However, it is not a voyage of shadows fading into eternal darkness. The soul is immortal. Death is not an end, merely a changing of place. For, as one day's end is the next day's beginning, we are assured that beyond the dark, beyond the well-earned sleep, there is light and a new sunrise.

Reborn in the Otherworld, we begin the reciprocal to this life and balance out our time here with a life in which the spirit is predominant and readily accepted. There we work toward an understanding of and balance with the material. So, when the full cycle is complete, we are ready to return to this world to start on a new phase of our journey.

This cycle is much like the turning of the day, which has two phases - daylight and night-time. It is difficult to say which of the worlds is represented by night and which by day. Although the Otherworld is often considered a land of summer stars, when compared with the shadow world in which we live it is also one of bright daylight.

As with much else, it is a matter of perspective. And although the denizens of each world may find the other worlds perplexing, there is no doubt that they are inextricably linked – the common medium being ourselves and all other living beings.

Belief in the immortality of the soul was exceedingly strong amongst ancestral Celts. It made them fierce warriors, for they had little fear of death. However, they were not reckless, because they also knew they had responsibilities.

The notion of personal responsibility and the immortality of the soul combined in the practice of some Celts accepting the repayment of debts being held over to the next life. Inherent in this is the belief that we travel together. That is, we are reborn amongst the same people. Our relationships may be different, but our responsibilities remain.

Some have taken this to be an indication that both our ancestors and modern Druids believe in a form of karma. This is not so. To begin with, although debts could be held over for repayment in the next life, this was not a widespread practice. It was a personal agreement that could be made between two individuals. It has nothing to do with accumulating brownie points with which to improve one's lot the next time round.

Such an idea is alien to the Celtic metaphysic. Responsibility for one's actions lies with the self in the here and now. Responsibility for one's actions is an inherent quality of those actions. You do something and you take responsibility for it because it is right to do so, not because there is a reward of some description involved, be that heaven, a better life, or nirvana.

Some will point to Celtic tales in which people lead many lives as different animals. Most of these tales are about shapeshifting. Those that do indicate that souls are reborn as animals through a number of cycles are exceptions rather than the norm – which is why they feature in these wonder tales. And even if they were the norm, they cannot be taken as an indication that punishment for being bad is to return as a 'lower' life form. Animals are not 'lower' life forms. They are our equals. Many of them are teachers; all of them are guides.

That there is a way to move on from this cycle of rebirth is also beyond doubt. The Celtic metaphysic is based on Truth and a search for the balance between the material and the spiritual. In our case, that means increasing our understanding and integration of our spiritual natures. Having achieved that balance, we are well placed to become teachers (as humans or in animal form) in these worlds before looking to master other aspects of being in places and times beyond our current comprehension.

An understanding of the balance between the material and spiritual can be seen in our ancestors' custom of burying personal belongings along with the bodies of those that owned them. This is often taken to be a primitive expression of the belief that you can take it with you.

In a sense this is true, but not in the crude way that most commentators imply. All things are imbued with spirit, even lumps of rock. Personal items such as jewellery, weapons, professional tools, games, and the like, all become endowed with the spirit of their owner through prolonged use and close personal contact. They are an integral part of who that person is. This was particularly so in a society in which personal material possessions were few in number and long-lasting.

Such items cannot be passed on to others. The pattern of the spirit of their original owner is too deeply embedded in their being for them to be transferred to anyone else. This is especially true of any item that is used in ritual. That is why a Druid should ask that their ceremonial equipment is buried or cremated with them - hence the need to use only natural materials.

Not only can others not use them, but they are also, as already stated, integral to the person who owned them. They derive their spirit from a given person, but that person also has their spirit shaped by the personal objects they possess. The same is true for relationships. We are shaped in large part by those people, animals, and landscapes with which we have close and prolonged contact. This is true for our spirit and for our spiritual understanding as well. To move to the Otherworld (or back to this) without that wider spiritual endowment is to be reborn incomplete, is to be held back on our new journey.

Reverence for our ancestors (and the ability to communicate with them) becomes a great deal easier to understand in light of this. We are our ancestors. Not, perhaps, the previous generation or two (although our journeys can sometimes be pitiably short in the worlds), but we are now in the strange position in our media rich world of being able to look at photographs and film of people who may once have been us.

The search for past life experiences is not one to be encouraged. It is a waste of this life. As is an undue emphasis on the notion of karma; of living in the shadow of what our past lives may have been like and how we might influence the next. We are here today to live today.

This does not mean we should not live in right fashion. Living in the now is not divorced from an understanding of the past or a care for the future. Indeed, living in the now by the tenets of the Celtic metaphysic demands, somewhat paradoxically, that our concerns and responsibilities take all the worlds at all times into account.

The Otherworld

Of all the diverse worlds we mention, it is the Otherworld that is of most concern to us. This is the place to which our souls migrate when our bodies die to enjoy there a new life; and from whence they come that we may be reborn once more in this world.

The Otherworld is not a land of the dead. It is not a supernatural realm. Both concepts are alien to the Celtic metaphysic. These definitions have come about as the result of attempting to understand the Celtic view of the world by comparing it with the metaphysic of other peoples and of other times. Both worlds are natural. Both worlds are worlds of the living. They are contiguous one with another and, in places, they overlap.

The cycle that takes us from world to world through a series of rebirths is the normal way to make the journey. However, it is not the only way. The denizens of one world can visit other worlds and then, with care and luck, return to their own. Such an undertaking is not without extreme hazard, not least because it is all too easy to mistake the Otherworld for Faerie.

The three worlds we have mentioned fit together much as the three circles in this diagram:

There is an area common to all three and each overlaps with the other. It is, therefore, possible to move from one to the other without having to 'die', but the diagram should not be taken too literally. Whereas some religious traditions have well defined ideas of where one world ends and another begins (think of the pearly gates of the Christian Heaven), the Celtic notion is, quite in keeping with the Celtic metaphysic, extremely fluid. Each world flows into the other and there are times when the gateways and crossing points are easier to find and use than others.

Nor should it be taken to mean that there are just the three worlds. There are many, and there is an ancient tradition of voyaging in search of these other lands. The *immram* was a quest in which whatever was sought was attained not just through physical prowess and endurance, but also through wisdom and a testing of the soul. Such was the power of these tales that they were adopted into the Christian tradition both as *immrama* and in much altered form as the Grail quest.

Many wonderful lands and islands are mentioned in these tales, each a world in its own right, and they are reached by sailing strange seas in the West. They range from the truly bizarre to those places that might easily be mistaken for this world. Of all those visited, only one is the world to which our souls migrate to be reborn.

No matter how unusual they may seem, none of these worlds is supernatural. Supernatural is a meaningless term. It means beyond or outside the natural. As the natural is a term meaning the whole, the universe, there can be nothing beyond or outside that. The Otherworld, Faerie, and all the other realms are simply places and conditions beyond our full understanding. This does not mean they are fantasies or non-existent.

Unfortunately, we live in a world in which scientific materialism has come to dominate our thinking and our institutions. Talk of or belief in (or a statement of knowledge about) a place like the Otherworld is considered with contempt. Yet the personal experience of those who are open to the whole of reality (rather than the small portion lorded over by materialists) is that the Otherworld and Faerie are real places and that their denizens are as interested in us as we are in them.

The Otherworld is a mirror of this world. Moreover, this world is seen by each of us through our own eyes and interpreted by each of us in ways unique to us. The mirror of this vision we each have of the world is, therefore, unique to us as well. Our experience of the Otherworld (and of Faerie) will have much in common with that of anyone else who has been there, but it will also have much that is different.

Again, this is often used to denigrate the experience as fantasy. If these are real places, say detractors, why do we not all experience them the same. Well, how much of this world have you seen? Moreover, how much of those pieces that you have seen are the same now as when you saw them last? And is your experience the same as those you were with when you visited?

If you have not journeyed to the Otherworld, it is difficult to visualize what it might be like. The easiest way to think of it is to call to mind the places and times in which you were happiest and most at peace. These are not the superficial or fleeting moments of fun that we all experience. The feeling is much deeper, those times when you have felt at one with the world about you, when the peace within you was such that you could sink wholly into the universe and stand proud of it at one and the same time. A mystical experience.

Those are times when you stand close to or within the boundaries of the Otherworld. That is what it is like there. These experiences allow us a glimpse because we are most in tune with the way of the Otherworld at these times.

It is also a place of balance, countering the Outworld that we currently inhabit. There are, for example, no cities to be found there, as we would recognize the term. Cities are manifestations of the materialistic way in which we live. Civilization (literally 'living in cities') has brought with it as necessary concomitants the likes of war, famine, ecological destruction, crime, poverty, disease, and an erosion of the spiritual side of human existence.

Our lives there are lived in spirit and our life's task is to come to understand the material side of our existence so that we may better cope with it when we are incarnate in this world. The mirror of this is true when we are here, for now our life's work is to understand better our spiritual side so that when we move to the Otherworld we can concentrate on understanding our material being. And in both worlds, we strive for order and for balance.

It is when we understand fully these aspects of ourselves and have achieved balance that we move beyond this cycle to a new one. What that is and how it works is well beyond us and need not concern us. To worry about that would be to neglect what we are here for.

Our journeys back and forth come in two forms. When our material form dies as all material forms do, the soul moves to a place on the shore. All souls gather here and are then ferried across the Western Ocean by the likes of Barinthus and Bíle, deities whose honoured task it is to conduct souls between the worlds. We have little choice in this, as it is the natural order of things.

Many people fear death, yet there is no need. The material body dies, and that process can be uncertain. Fear of pain, loss of control, loss of dignity are all understandable. We all face them. They are inevitable aspects of the decay of the material side of our being. Yet death itself, the moving on of the soul, is merely the start of a new journey. It is the sunset, with the promise of a new day inherent in the demise of the old.

It is why we celebrate a death as the beginning of a new life. We are right to mourn for the loss of a loved one. It is painful for us to see them suffer (especially if their lives are prolonged for the sake of it); it is painful coping with the wound caused by their amputation from our lives. Yet we should never lose sight of the fact that mourning and grief are for our benefit, part of the healing process.

Those who have passed on to their journey to the Otherworld do not need our tears. In fact, obsessive mourning, an unwillingness to let go is unhealthy and unnatural. It does us great harm because we cease to live our own lives properly. It does the departed harm, as they cannot move on as they must; move on to a world where they deserve and need to be.

When we lose loved ones in this world, we must remember them, give thanks for having had the chance to share time with them, and celebrate their existence. And one of the best ways of doing that is to move on. We will meet them again and we can celebrate them each year at Samhain.

Of course, there is another way in which we can travel to the Otherworld. This, however, is not to be recommended to anyone unless they are extremely experienced and know precisely what they are doing. Even then, it is not something we would endorse. The whole enterprise is fraught with danger. That our soul makes the journey on the demise of our material being is one thing. To attempt it in corporeal form is quite another. We should certainly read of and meditate on the journeys of others. However, we must remember that they were great heroes imbued with prodigious amounts of strength, courage, and wisdom – and often even that was not enough. Arthur made the journey with a number of heroic companions. Of all those who went (three shiploads) only seven returned and even then it is not entirely certain that they gained the prize they sought.

The Otherworld is not our natural realm when we are incarnate in this world. Moreover, Faerie is not our natural realm whether we are incarnate in this world or the Other. To travel to these places puts us in great danger. Caution and experience can assist us, but even then, they are not absolute guarantees of our safety. Nor should we confuse working with our ancestors with travelling to the Otherworld. When we consult with our ancestors, it is done with their consent at times when and places where the worlds are coexistent.

Samhain is, of course, the best known of times for this – sadly corrupted into a foolish excuse for some children (and adults) to demand we pay for protection against their threats. However, we can consult our ancestors at other times and places – the reason why so many people need to know where their loved ones are buried or their ashes are scattered. Many people talk to their dear ones at their grave. It does not mean they believe that person is there, but it is a ritual that enables them to open themselves up and continue the conversations they had when both were still in this world.

This aspect of connection with the Otherworld is harmless and, in some degree, to be encouraged provided it does not become obsessive. Keeping open the dialogue we had, helps to keep alive the memory of those people as well as allowing us to tap into their wisdom. 'What would Granny have done?' is a more potent question than many imagine - especially if you all knew Granny well. Her wisdom continues to live in you and she is quite capable of adding to that from her new existence. She has not incarnated in the Otherworld as your Granny, but her soul continues and is well aware of its responsibilities and obligations to the family and to the tribe, even when the concept of tribe has become lost within the other social constructs of our time.

The great voyage that we will all make (and have already made on many occasions) is of great importance to us. So, too, is our connection with our ancestors. But our hunger for an understanding of what is to come and of the places to which we will eventually travel should not divert us from our real work, or from the place in which that work is to be done – the here and the now. Sunsets may be spectacular and linger in our memory, but they only last for a tiny fraction of the day. Moreover, if we spent all our time waiting in anticipation of them, the rest of the day would be wasted. Treasure each moment. When the sun does finally touch the western horizon, your joy of it will be all the greater for knowing that it is the glory that crowns a day well spent.

PART FOUR

A CRANE BAG

GLOSSARY

Many works of this nature are liberally scattered with capital letters. We have attempted to stick to the convention of using them only to denote proper nouns and to differentiate between the everyday or generic use of a term and a specialized use that points to a symbolic and/or spiritual element.

athame (see **wand**)

awen - inspiration or divine power, an energy flow or communion. It is also the poetic muse, the breath of creativity, even the reins that bind us to the source of all inspiration. All these meanings derive from the root *awen*, still extant in the Welsh language, meaning 'poetic gift', making it bardic in nature – the gift of Cerridwen's cauldron. Druids chant it, mantra style, to give themselves focus and to raise a flow of creative and healing energies.

cauldron – a sacred object that offers nourishment, healing, and wisdom to those who partake of its contents. It is also a vessel of rebirth. In ancient tales, various cauldrons were used to revive the dead. It is a symbol that has evolved over the centuries, most notably as the Grail.

celebration – the performance of ritual and ceremony to mark or honour a specific event or person.

ceremony - a formal act or series of acts prescribed by ritual, protocol, or convention.

chalice – a cup or goblet used specifically for ritual purposes.

deiseal/tuathal – deiseal, often given in its Anglicized form of 'deosil', means 'sunwise' and is the preferred direction in druidic working. Tuathal (anticlockwise or widdershins) is the direction used for unwinding energies. This does not make tuathal a 'bad' direction although it should be used only to close ceremonies.

festival – a series of formal and/or informal events in celebration of an idea, place, time, or person. Embedded in this may be a formal ceremony, but it will also include feasting, music, dance, and the opportunity for a good gossip.

Forest/forest – Forest with a capital 'F' is used to denote the inner landscape of the Druid as well as being a metaphor for the world of spirit, whilst forest with a small 'f' is used to name a collection of trees.

Goddess - the Goddess can mean many different things to people. In the Celtic pantheon, there are many types of goddess, all with tales of wonder and wisdom to impart. In Her primal aspect as the Great Goddess, we see Her as a universal triple Goddess of all nature. She is the maiden, mother, and cailleach. We know Her as Danu who gives life as the breath of spring, the fullness of the harvest. She is the death and rebirth of the year, our lives, and the universe. She is the Land, the Sea, and the Sky. She is the mighty ocean, the silvery brook, the Moon, the stars, the dark deep forests, the poppy filled meadow, She is life. As Druids, we honour Her in our daily lives, meditations, and rituals.

God – the God, in Celtic tradition, is the consort of the Goddess. He is generally associated with birth and death and often helps to ferry souls between the worlds. He is not to be confused with the concept of deity advocated by monotheistic religions.

magic – Druid magic is somewhat different from that used in other pagan paths. Druids do not cast spells or make potions. Instead, they work with the natural energies around them. This energy is found in all things - animals, trees, stones, birds, water, weather, sound, even dreams. In ritual and meditation, they link into these energies and work with them for the good, giving out love, light, and healing.

metaphysics - The study of the ultimate causes and underlying nature of things, especially the nature of being. A particular world view is known as a 'metaphysic'. The word derives from Aristotle's work, the *Metaphysics,* so called because it was written after (*meta*) his work on the physical world (*physics*). It is now generally taken to mean 'beyond the physical'.

protection - Druids do not believe in evil demons and devils. What Druids protect themselves against are the negative, exhausting energies that are abundant in our ailing world. Healing work is especially draining and we need to ensure we do not deplete ourselves. That is why it is important to work within a circle and to close it properly afterwards. The same goes for making sure you are properly grounded after working.

ritual - the form or order of words prescribed for a ceremony.

scrying – a method of divination in which events are discerned by gazing at or into a reflective surface.

staff (see **wand**)

tuathal (see **deiseal**)

wand - made from wood, wands are used for directing energies when casting a circle or as symbols during specific rituals. They are a continuation of a Druid's relationship with tree spirits. A wand is normally about eighteen inches in length – that is, from your elbow to your fingertips. It can be of any kind of wood, although each type has its own energies, so you might decide to have more than one. You will need to study the properties of trees and their relation to such things as ogham before you decide.

An athame is a double-edged knife. It is never used to cut anything in the material plane and the blade should be kept blunt. Although considered a Craft tool, a number of Druids use them. A word of warning. The Police can consider these offensive weapons, even if they are blunt. Being caught in possession of them can lead to prosecution. If you intend to use them in public ritual or in a public place, it is best to seek legal advice.

The Druid's staff is more decorative than practical. Although they can be used for ritual purposes, including circle casting, they can be a bother when you are in a circle and you need to link hands, or when getting to a ritual using public transport!

world/World – The word 'world' (with a small 'w') is generally interchangeable with the word 'universe' and means 'everything that is'. It can also be used to mean 'everything on the planet'. When 'World' (with a capital 'W') is used, it has a specialized meaning – 'the physical, ideological, and social constructs of human beings'. Druids work to mitigate the harm caused to the world by the World.

BOOK LIST

Ritual is about making your own connection with the sacred. We have offered guidance in these pages, but in the end, the rituals you use must be your own. The books listed below may help you in your research.

Ellis, P.B. (1994), *The Druids*, Constable, London.

Green, M. (1988), *The Path through the Labyrinth*, Thoth, Loughborough.

Jones, K. (1991), *The Ancient British Goddess*, Ariadne Publications, Glastonbury.

MacCulloch, J.A. (1911), *The Religion of the Ancient Celts*, Constable, London.

MacKillop, J. (1998), *Dictionary of Celtic Mythology*, Oxford University Press, Oxford.

Maier, B. (1997), *Dictionary of Celtic Religion and Culture*, Boydell, Woodbridge.

Markale, J. (1999), *The Druids*, Inner Traditions, Rochester, Vermont.

Mason, P. & Franklin, A. (1998), *The Sacred Circle Tarot*, Llewellyn, St Paul, MN.

Matthews, C. (2001), *The Celtic Book of the Dead*, Grange Books, Rochester, Kent.

Mathews, C. & J. (1992), *Ladies of the Lake*, Thorsons, London.

Mathews, C. & J. (1997), *Hallowquest*, Thorsons, London.

Mathews, C. & J. (1999), *The Celtic Spirit*, HarperCollins, London.

Rolleston, T.W. (1911), *Myths and Legends of the Celtic Race*, Constable, London.

Ross, A. (1992), *Pagan Celtic Britain*, Constable, London.

Sjoestedt, M. (1949), *Gods and Heroes of the Celts*, Methuen, London.

Squire, C. (1905), *Celtic Myth and Legend*, Newcastle, Van Nuys.

Stewart, R.J. (1990), *Celtic Gods, Celtic Goddesses*, Blandford, London.

Lightning Source UK Ltd.
Milton Keynes UK

175465UK00001B/10/A